The Girl Who Cried Love

The Girl Who Cried Love

A Pivot to Self-Worth

Lindsay Manfredi

Published by Best Seller Publishing®, St. Augustine, FL
Best Seller Publishing® is a registered trademark.
Printed in the United States of America.

ISBN: 978-1-969338-68-7

This publication is designed to provide accurate and authoritative information with regard to the subject matter covered. It is sold with the understanding that the publisher is not engaged in rendering legal, accounting, or other professional advice. If legal advice or other expert assistance is required, the services of a competent professional should be sought. The opinions expressed by the author in this book are not endorsed by Best Seller Publishing® and are the sole responsibility of the author rendering the opinion.

For more information, please write:
Best Seller Publishing®
1775 US-1 #1070
St. Augustine, FL 32084
or call 1 (626) 765-9750

Visit us online at: www.BestSellerPublishing.org

THIS BOOK IS DEDICATED TO ALL OF US
WHO HAVE LOOKED FOR LOVE IN ALL THE
WRONG PLACES.

Table of Contents

Introduction

We all know the story of the boy who cried wolf. Time after time, in his mischievous delight, the shepherd boy would shout, "WOLF, WOLF!" down the hillside to the villagers below. Each time, they came running, only to find no wolf. Frustrated, they returned to the village. After a few false alarms, the day finally came when a real wolf appeared. The boy cried out for help—but no one came. His flock scattered. He was officially screwed.

When he asked a villager why no one responded, the answer was simple: "Nobody believes a liar, even when he's telling the truth."

Sometimes, I feel like my love life mirrors that story. I'd declare, with certainty, that "this person is the one," only to watch it fall apart. It felt like people were whispering, *"There goes Lindsay, falling in love again... let's see how long this one lasts."*

But I don't doubt for a second that what I felt wasn't real. I'm a lover. I've loved deeply—people, moments, music, life. I love it all. My friends remind me that this loving, nurturing, excited, and accepting part of me is something special. But it's also what has led to my heartbreak, time and time again. Sometimes, there have been times I called it love when it was really just love of the idea of love. Still, every person who's crossed my path taught me something that shaped who I am today.

This isn't a sad story. Sure, there have been sad chapters—even during the writing of this book, as I held tightly onto a dream only to watch it crumble. But this is a story of hope. It's a story of love. It's a story of pivoting. Not the fairy tale kind of love, not the polished, perfect kind. It's the hope of finding what I was really searching for: love within myself.

There are always two sides to every story. Neither is right or wrong—just different perspectives. Just like love. We are shaped by how we were raised, how we experience loss, how we've experienced trauma, and how we heal. Growth begins when we choose to stay open. When we learn to pivot back to love.

In Jillian Turecki's, *It Begins With You*, she writes:

"The relationship we have with ourselves is the most important relationship we will ever have, and we will have to continuously work on that relationship to break through the barriers that prevent us from true emotional intimacy with another person."

So many of us miss that mark. Love is the theme of nearly every story, song, and film—and yet we struggle to truly understand it. I know I have. That's why I'm writing this book. I hope my story inspires you, because I've missed the mark more times than I can count.

This is a one-sided account of my past—relationships, heartbreaks, awakenings—that led me to a deeper, evolving love. A love I began to find when I started loving myself for who I was, who I am, and who I'm becoming. Self-love is a daily choice. It's not always easy. I've probably let myself down more than anyone else. But I'm finally starting to see the patterns I was oblivious to before.

Most of my life, I looked for love in all the wrong places. Because looking outside ourselves is easier. Because it's comforting to believe that someone else will save us. Esther Perel puts it best in *Mating in Captivity*:

"Today, we look to one person to provide what an entire village once did: a sense of grounding, meaning, and continuity."

When you see it that way, it's no wonder so many of us feel disappointed. It's no wonder more people are choosing to stay single and are throwing up their hands in frustration.

So, I'm writing this for both of us. To face the expectations, fears, and patterns I've had to dismantle. To show you how I began setting boundaries, confronting self-sabotage, choosing a year of sobriety, and finding strength in the love and support of my people.

Truth is messy. Sometimes I wonder if our ugliest parts are meant to be shared or do we keep them sacred? I used to think no one could love my darkness when I barely knew how to love it myself. Some days, I still struggle. I wonder which truths are mine to hold and which can be handed over. Is healing a battle or an act of surrender? What happens when we stop trying to rewrite the past and start becoming who we're meant to be?

Every messy chapter led me here. To a love that feels hopeful and human. Inside and out.

Writing this has been hard. This is me, unfiltered. The stories that follow shaped me—from childhood to now. I'm sharing them so you know: you're not alone. Love is complicated. But when we turn inward, we begin to break the cycles. I'm finally ready to end mine. There are no names, only a letter representing the story it belongs to. I do name my friends. There could also be some triggering subject matters for some. But all of this is true.

While writing this, I was also editing the audiobook for *Unfuck-withable: A Guide to Inspired Badassery*. I'm proud of that book. It helped people. It changed lives. But I also know I didn't go deep enough. I talked about *what* to do, without unpacking *why* it's so hard. I didn't speak enough about trauma or the invisible weight we carry. I sometimes oversimplified the journey.

And the truth? It's rarely simple.

I've compared myself to other writers. I've questioned my impact. Even with all the messages from readers saying it helped—that it made a difference—I still wondered if I did enough or if I was good enough.

Maybe that's because I'm still learning. I'm still healing. I'm still working on my confidence. And I'm trying to honor how far I've come. Writing a book is hard. Writing one that opens your wounds for the world to see? That's something else entirely.

This book is about rebuilding. About asking hard questions: What do I value? What kind of love do I deserve? What old stories am I still carrying? Why have I held onto people that hurt me to my core?

Some stories in here are hard to tell. Some still carry shame. But I'm owning them. They shaped me. And while I regret some of the harm I've caused, I'm learning to offer myself grace. I'm learning to forgive. And I'm learning to understand the roots of my choices.

Artists create from fire. From friction. We just want to matter. Maybe this book will help someone else. Maybe it's helping me.

So here it is: My truth. My beginning again on multiple occasions.

I hope you find pieces of yourself in these pages. I hope something in here helps you recognize your own patterns and red flags, especially if you're in a relationship that doesn't feel right. I hope it reminds you of your worth—and that you don't need to earn it. And I hope you stay open, even when it's hard. Because that's where the healing begins. There is always room to grow. There is always room to come home to yourself.

Let's begin.

All my love,

Lindsay

CHAPTER 1

The Inner Child

I believe the way we love is rooted deeply in how we were raised and the relationships we had with our parents or caregivers, along with what we experienced around us. As humans, we crave love and connection from the beginning. That's nothing new—there's plenty of research to back it up. I longed for love, attention, and validation growing up. Hell, I still do. That may never go away. But where I seek it now has changed.

Roots

I grew up in a very religious home in the small town of Kokomo, Indiana with my mother, my father and my two older sisters. Each of us four years apart in age. I am the youngest. The only man consistently in my life was my father. All my grandparents and male relatives lived out of state, and I wasn't close with any of them. I'd see some of them once or twice a year for holidays, but that was about it. And as for my father—growing up, I didn't know if I loved him or hated him.

He was a right-wing "Christian" man. His love often came packaged as control. Any questioning or rebellion was met with anger, spankings (it was the '80s, after all), revoked privileges, or biting down on a bar of soap. Not swallowing it—but biting it. Who came up with that punishment? Whoever it was... they sucked. I'd never do that to a child, but back then, it was normal.

After the punishment would come the "I love you," and "This is why I do this to you." Insert any "bad behavior" here. So, in my child-mind: if I wasn't doing the right "thing" *all* the time, I got punished. It was my fault. I was "bad." That's likely where my people-pleasing and rebellion took root and became ongoing patterns my entire life. Do right, get praised. Do wrong, get punished.

I never felt close to my father. He was always working, running (literally—he was an avid jogger), at choir rehearsal, or zoned out in front of the news, some evangelical show or watching sports, all while re-modeling our home while we lived there. It was normal to have walls knocked down in rooms for weeks and months at a time. But if I'm being honest, there was no real connection in our family. And yes, many people have grown up without a father at all—so I do acknowledge the privilege of his presence. He did what he could. But that doesn't erase how absent he felt to me emotionally.

Add in Christian school and church three times a week, and you've got a cocktail of fear-based doctrine. There was no space for mistakes. No conversations. Just authoritarian rules and the looming fear of disappointing God, going to hell—or worse, making our parents look bad. I didn't feel like our behavior was about our growth. I felt like it was about their reputation.

My father is not that same man today. I know now he did the best he could with the tools he had. Ego, trauma, and emotional intelligence weren't dinner-table topics in evangelical homes. I share all of this because I've realized, as an adult, I've carried patterns that held me back. The fear of being judged, abandoned, or rejected made me hide parts of myself. It's something I'm still unlearning.

Sex was never discussed. At all. It was taboo. The message was clear: no sex until marriage. If you did, it was a sin. And if you sinned, you'd be punished. I learned more about sex in third grade from my best friend's older sister than I ever did at home.

Born in 1978, I grew up in the '80s and '90s. We didn't talk about relationships or emotions. Everything I learned about love came from music, movies, magazines, and TV. I was curious. A tomboy. I chased boys on the playground. I liked attention and knew I liked boys early on.

We had family friends from church with two sons, and our families spent a lot of time together. Backyard BBQs. Tree climbing. Choir rehearsals. Lots of unsupervised time. One day, that curiosity led to a "show me yours, I'll show you mine" moment. I don't even remember who suggested it, probably me. But someone told a parent, and I was punished. No conversation. No context. Just shame.

That was my first real lesson in shame.

I remember being in the bathtub and realizing it felt good under the faucet—without knowing what an orgasm was. I was probably around 8 or 9 years-old when my sister's best friend caught me and threatened to tell on me, laughing and mocking me. More shame. More secrecy. Still, no guidance. I was on my own.

Not long after, my oldest sister, Heather, was off to college, so it was just Tiffany and me. We were latch-key kids as you would call it. Both my parents worked full-time, so we were pretty much left to fend for ourselves. My middle sister went through her own little rebellious phase. She and her best friend started smoking cigarettes and would share with me so I wouldn't tell on them. I loved it. I felt cool. That also wasn't the first time I had smoked: A friend and I from church would spend long Sunday afternoons during those unsupervised choir rehearsals, digging through her dad's car ashtray, lighting up half-smoked cigarettes. I know: Gross.

I knew from a very young age I wanted love. I wanted to be chosen. I wanted to feel the way it looked in the movies. And when you combine that longing with no guidance, you get a kid who learns from the world instead of from within.

I also learned betrayal very early on: The circle of girlfriends in my grade school were mean girls. One day, they'd be your friend, the next day, you were out. With no explanation besides, *"You know what you did,"* never truly knowing what I did. I knew to keep my mouth shut when it came to gossiping. The other girls would do it. I would not. Just being there was enough to pin something on you. And some of the parents were even worse. I would be popular some days, and other days, I would be the outcast. There would be no consistency, which would cause underlying trust issues throughout my life, along with trying to prove I was worthy to those who bullied me.

At home, because I was the youngest, my sisters didn't really want me around. The annoying little sister. They would call me "Lindsay Joy, which you are not," because my middle name is Joy. I often felt like an outcast.

As I got a little older, my friend group changed a bit, and I became even more sexually curious. We'd have sleepovers where we'd spend the entire night loading up on sugar, giggling, and making out with pillows to learn how to kiss. It was also not uncommon to touch each other and rub up on each other. My curiosity with sex was certainly not out of the norm. However, I would be the first to get "experience" of everyone in my group of friends. My first real kiss was in the 6th grade. And it was messy, wet, and gross.

So, it's no surprise I lost my virginity at thirteen. I met a 17-year-old at the mall—because that's where we went in the '90s. I thought I was in love. He made me feel special. He gave me attention. I loved being kissed because he was a *good* kisser, much better than my first experience. Within weeks, I was in a trailer park, on a waterbed, in front of his dog named D-O-G, losing my virginity. It was painful, awkward, and probably not even successful.

I don't remember feeling heartbroken. I just moved on. To the next. And the next. I was searching for someone—anyone—to see me. Choose me. Validate me.

Around the time, which was the summer after losing my virginity, my middle sister and I transitioned from the private school we attended, to a public school, Taylor High School. My parents were building a house in that school district, so I was moving for the first time in my life. Plus, I was finally going to a public school which meant I didn't have to wear dresses every day. I was thrilled. My sister was going into her senior year. I was going into the 8th grade. The boy I had lost my virginity too also attended this high school. It was a little weird seeing him again, but it didn't really affect me. He had a serious girlfriend, and we never spoke.

I tried out for the volleyball team and made it. I was good at sports. My sister also played, so it was one love we shared. I began making some friends at my new school and we would sneak around and smoke cigarettes after practice. It was the thing back then. While I wasn't a fan of school, I was a good student who had always gotten good grades.

Bullying at this school began early on. I didn't understand what was wrong with me. I'd brush it off and try to get along with everyone, giving my time and patience to those who did not deserve it, just to fit in.

At fourteen, I was sexually molested by my great uncle. I kept it to myself for years. Eventually, I told my aunt, and she helped me tell my parents. They were mortified, as you can imagine. We discussed the implications it would have on my grandmother and the rest of the family. Ultimately, the decision to oust him was up to me. My parents were going to back me. I decided it was best to sweep it under the rug to keep the family together. He was old. He would die soon. There was nothing I could do about the past, so I continued living my life. There was too much shame surrounding it.

I quit volleyball soon after and set my sights on Color Guard. I was a natural and fell in love with it. But something tragic happened: One evening, I convinced a friend from church to let me drive her car in the neighborhood. I turned in front of a boy on a moped, sending him flying off. He was in the hospital for weeks. He had steel rods put in his legs, broke so many bones. It was like living in a nightmare. I had never been truly sorry about anything in my life up until this point. The feeling from causing bodily harm to someone was about as low as I could get. His family forgave me. He forgave me. He eventually recovered but his life would never be the same. He tragically passed many years later from a drug overdose, and I couldn't help but wonder if it was all my fault. More guilt. More shame. Only this time, everyone knew.

Teenage years were brutal, and my decision-making was worse. I couldn't imagine what it would have been like if we had cell phones and social media back then. I ended up getting kicked out of color guard for smoking a cigarette in the bathroom of the Chicago Bears stadium when we were performing at a halftime show. I was a mess inside and tried to keep it together outside. My parents didn't know what to do with me.

With extracurricular school activities on the backburner, I baby-sat often and was constantly hit on by grown men—fathers of the children I was watching or their friends. I was still a child, but the adult attention made me feel... something. Wanted, maybe. Important. But now? It makes my stomach turn. I knew from all the attention I was getting that I was a pretty girl yet felt very ugly inside.

I eventually had a sexual relationship with a high school boyfriend. My parents found out. A meeting happened with his parents. And that was that. Again, no real conversations. Just consequences. Always about sin. Never about self-worth.

So yeah, my rebellion followed the cliché: sex, drugs, and rock 'n' roll. But I didn't want to be numb. I wanted to feel alive. I wanted to feel something. I was sent to therapists and psychiatrists and was diagnosed with bipolar and manic depression by sixteen. Medicated with Depakote and Prozac, I became a ghost of myself. I don't even remember when I stopped taking the meds. I just ran away. Literally, which I'll share in the next chapter.

I never knew how incredibly lost I was and how powerfully my experiences and decisions would affect me throughout my life.

I am very close with my family now, especially my mother. Parenting has changed since then. At least, I hope it has. I see so many parts of my childhood that were wrapped in guilt, shame and people pleasing, leading to a downward spiral. I'm a parent now, to a trans child named Chev. Before we even understood his gender identity, his father and I agreed we'd always talk openly about sex and curiosity. When he got his first iPhone, I took him out to dinner. We talked about porn. He admitted he'd seen it. And we had an open, shame-free conversation about it.

Curiosity is normal. So is pleasure. So is confusion. I wanted my kid to know that. I didn't want Chev growing up with the shame I did. I wanted him to have space to ask questions, feel safe, and be seen. I'm grateful he didn't follow my path.

Bottom line? I was a girl who wanted to be seen. Loved. Chosen. Would I ever find my happily ever after?

CHAPTER 2

The Abusive One
— Him | The Savior — Me

I met who I considered my first real love at a Narcotics Anonymous meeting. I'd had boyfriends in high school, but something always gave me the ick. They'd say or do something, and I'd be done. I was never in love—just craving attention and going through the motions, completely disconnected from who I was or what I wanted.

If you read my first book, you know I spent most of my sophomore and junior years in and out of juvenile detention. Running away became my MO because, at the time, I genuinely hated my parents, and I hated being drug to church every Sunday. Also, I really *wanted* to do what I wanted to do. It was not uncommon for my friends and I to sneak out of whoever's house we were staying at and meet up with boys. We were all sexually active by then, sharing stories of conquests.

The first time I ran away, I was gone for a week and a half. My friend Alice had just moved, so I stayed with her, her mom and older brother in Rochester, Indiana. Her mom didn't care what we did. I eventually felt bad and called home. When Alice brought me back, the police were waiting. I was arrested for truancy and placed on

probation. Not long after, I skipped town again to attend Lollapa-
looza to see the band, Hole. When I came back, I spent an entire
day scrubbing walls at the youth center with a toothbrush, with *Ma-
chinehead* by Bush, blaring on repeat in my headphones. To this day,
when I hear that song, it takes me back there.

Rules meant nothing to me. I was a runaway, a rebel, a teenager
spiraling.

Skipping school got me arrested again. My parents were done
trying to manage me. The first time I was locked up, it was in the
unsecure section of Kinsey Youth Center. I would live at the center during the week, would get transported to and from school, and
could go home on weekends. That period changed me. I was newly
prescribed Prozac and Depakote. And while it helped to mask some
of the guilt from the accident I had caused, I emotionally flatlined.
Music became my anchor.

Pearl Jam's *Vitalogy* had just dropped, and I obsessed with the
song, *Tremor Christ*. I'd pray it would come on the radio during my
drives. That song was everything. Smashing Pumpkins' *Pisces Iscar-
iot* was on repeat when I was home on weekends. I didn't even know
the song, *Landslide*, was a Fleetwood Mac cover at the time, but at
sixteen, those lyrics hit deep. When everything was crumbling, music saved me.

The '90s grunge scene was my lifeline: Nirvana, Hole, Sound-
garden, STP, Alice in Chains, Garbage, Bush. Films like *Singles, Natural Born Killers, Dazed and Confused*—all of it shaped me. We had
no cell phones. No social media. Just our imaginations, our music,
and our rebellion. We created our own worlds, and that was survival.

Eventually, my parents stopped paying for my detention. They
sent me to rehab instead because it was covered by insurance. Because I was on probation, I was court-ordered to attend NA meet-
ings. Turns out, I didn't hate it. I could chain-smoke cigarettes, drink
coffee with adults, and vent about life.

That's where I met him.

K was beautiful. He went to a different school in a neighboring town. He played guitar, and was strong, sensitive, dark, and mysterious. We liked the same music, cigarettes, and coffee. I was obsessed. He'd just gotten out of a relationship, and I made it my mission to become his girlfriend.

And I did.

Soon, I was skipping school again to hang out at his place. I became pregnant at seventeen. My continued probation violations landed me in the secure side of Kinsey—essentially jail for teens. I wore scrubs, couldn't leave, and shared space with crack dealers from Detroit. Honestly, all we did was sit around and play cards, and I got really good at Spades.

I miscarried while I was locked up. Everyone, including his mom and mine, seemed relieved. But we stayed together. I got my GED while I was in there, which was a year before I would have graduated. When I got out, at nearly eighteen, I moved in with him.

K was complicated. He struggled with severe depression, and I believed I could save him. I worked two jobs to help pay rent for our tiny place in Kokomo. His moods grew darker. He started using drugs heavily and became physically abusive. It started with pushing. I knew it wasn't right when he would pin me up against the wall and scream at me.

One evening, I took a hit of acid, which became my wake-up call. This drug made me see a different perspective. I saw my life for what it was and where it was headed if I were to stay. I decided to leave the very next day. I knew if K found out my plans, there would most certainly be consequences. So, when he was at work, I moved back into my parents' house. There I was, asking my family if I could come back to the one place, I'd spent years trying to escape. They welcomed me with open arms.

Even after I left, K didn't let go. He tried to break into my parents' house while I was there. He attempted to kick down the doors and dented them with a hammer. The police were called. That was the last time I saw him. Who knows what would have happened if he got in? I know now I was divinely protected, even though I didn't realize it then.

I don't know what fueled all his rage. I thought love would fix it. That he'd see his potential if I just loved him enough. But love doesn't heal someone who doesn't want to heal. It just breaks you both.

I managed to follow my intuition and get out. So many people stay in abusive relationships because they don't know better—because no one ever told them they deserve more. Or they fear the consequences of leaving. I'm so grateful that my parents didn't turn me away. They took me back, again and again, even when they didn't understand me. I put them through hell, but they still showed me so much grace.

For the record, as far as my previous relationship with K is concerned, I have no regrets. I know every wild, messy, gut-wrenching decision shaped who I am today. But I recognize that I ignored the warning signs. He was not a healthy person, and our relationship was unhealthy as a result. Speaking of warning signs: If your partner drives like a maniac while you're in the car, and you fear for your life, that is a massive red flag. That's abuse, too.

The CDC estimates that **about 41% of women** have experienced sexual violence, physical violence, or stalking by an intimate partner during their lifetime—with roughly **61 million women** affected by psychological aggression. (CDC, 2025)

What does this look like?

- **Physical violence** is when a person hurts or tries to hurt a partner by using physical force.
- **Sexual violence** is forcing or attempting to force a partner to take part in a sex act, sexual touching, or a non-physical sexual event (e.g., sexting) when the partner does not or cannot consent.

- **Stalking** is a pattern of repeated, unwanted attention and contact by a partner that causes fear or concern for one's own safety or the safety of someone close to the victim.
- **Psychological aggression** is the use of verbal and non-verbal communication with the intent to harm a partner mentally or emotionally or to exert control over a partner.

If you or someone you know is in an abusive relationship, I urge you to please seek help.

There are resources available for you. I know the thought of leaving may be scary, but staying in something unhealthy or potentially dangerous is not worth your life, literally and figuratively.

So much had happened, and I was ready to move forward and start over. I was working as a third key manager at a retail store, living at home, and partying with new friends. In a small town like mine, that was all there was to do. I started drinking more and hanging around people doing harder drugs like crank and coke. I loved the high. I hated the comedown. I remember being curled up on a stranger's floor thinking *I never want to feel like this again.* I felt so dirty and depressed. *What was I doing? Why was I here?* It was enough for me to stop.

I decided to focus all my attention on learning to play guitar. My dad's old classical Alverez was always lying around. One day, I picked it up, learned some chords from a Mel-Bay chord book, and started writing my own songs. I eventually linked up with a friend who played, and I did my first collaboration. We recorded the song on an old 8-track. I was so excited and proud of myself, and I really wanted to dive into music. I had found something creative and productive to do. I finally started to believe what people told me my whole life: I had talent. I was just never focused. I realized I could leave my hometown. There was more for me out there.

And I was going to find it.

But even as I picked up the guitar and started to believe in my own story, I had no idea how many more times I'd have to lose myself before I truly found what I was looking for.

CHAPTER 3

Baby Daddy

Around the time I started shifting away from the crowd I did drugs with, is when I met my trans son's father. He was a body piercer at a local tattoo shop. I went in with a friend who was getting pierced, and something about him hit me like lightning. Tattooed, confident, bad boy energy—completely magnetic. The next day, I went back and got my tongue pierced just to see him again. Then that evening, armed with a bottle of wine I had bought with a fake ID that somehow had my actual photo on it (shoutout to the pre-DMV computer days), I showed up at his hotel. I was convinced I could make him fall in love with me—and eventually, he did.

He had a two-year old from a previous relationship, and he'd just gotten out of a relationship where he and his ex-girlfriend had given a baby up for adoption. He was strong, yet heartbroken, and of course, I believed my love could fix him and make everything better. Patterns, anyone?

I may have felt deeply insecure, but I did have hella confidence. As I learned about his past, I couldn't shake the feeling that I didn't measure up to his ex. (This is still something I work on—choosing not to compare myself to anyone else.)

In an effort to stay close to him, I convinced him to let me apprentice as a body piercer. We even moved in together. For context, this was 25+ years ago. We were young, naive, and though he wasn't a good partner for me back then, he's become a great friend and father. We share a child and have built a solid friendship since.

Back then, though, he wasn't great with money. I kept trying to "save" him, covering tattoo shop expenses with my maxed-out credit cards. He always promised to pay me back. He never did. It all crumbled. We fought constantly. I was 19 when I finally left him and cut my losses—back to my parents' house I went.

I was devastated. The heartbreak crushed me. I sobbed in my mom's arms, confused, but I knew I had to move on. I got my body piercing certification and continued to work at the same shop, just on different days. He quickly started dating someone else, which was another punch in the gut. I hated him. I loved him. I hated him. But I kept working, kept saving money. I had to get out of Kokomo.

Lesson learned: don't lend money unless you can afford never to see it again. He didn't mean harm, he was just trying to survive, like we all were.

Soon after, my sister set me up on a blind date with her co-worker's brother. He resided in Terre Haute, IN. We met up and went to a bonfire and played music. I performed some of the songs I had written, and some locals suggested I move there and start a band. I visited for a weekend, landed a piercing job, and moved the next week—This was my first time moving out of Kokomo. I rented a room in a shared house. I was 20 at the time.

In Terre Haute, I formed my first band, NSA – short for No Strings Attached. I bought a Courtney Love Fender Venus electric guitar and an Eddie Van Halen 5150-combo amp. We played a few gigs at a local bar. I pierced full-time and drank a lot—I'd have lattes and bagels in the morning, beer at night. I gained 20 pounds. I had no idea how to take care of my body.

I wasn't health conscious. I didn't exercise. I just lived the rock n' roll life. I even got arrested twice in one month—once for sitting drunk in my car (not driving), for public intoxication and another time for being underage in a bar. Five grand later, I got it all expunged. Thank God for a good lawyer.

After six months, my bassist suggested we move to Gainesville, Florida, and start a new band. That made sense to me. Everyone around me drank constantly. I didn't even smoke weed anymore because it made me anxious. I drank and occasionally took MDMA alone while listening to music. The band, Tool was my go-to for this.

I saved up some money and traded in my car for a van, packed all my music gear, piercing equipment and clothes, and headed to Gainesville. The plan was to start fresh, and I was in love with the idea of it. I wanted to gain new experiences and start a band and make my mark on the music scene. I just needed to find the right people to do it with.

Me and my bassist stayed with his friends for about a month. All they did was sit around and drink malt liquor and reminisced about the past. I searched for piercing jobs but found nothing solid—there was only one sketchy shop in town.

Eventually, we moved into a new house. We had our own rooms with an extra room, and the house also had space for a rehearsal area. I found another roommate to help pay the rent and found our new bandmates. Meanwhile, my savings started to disappear. I got a job at a sandwich shop—Tom Petty allegedly worked there once.

But my bassist never got a job. He drank all day and never got serious about making music, so that took a back seat. Meanwhile, I met some girlfriends, celebrated my 21st, and rang in the new millennium. Rent was falling behind, and we hadn't written a single song. When the eviction came, I got a gas station job and crashed with a friend.

I sold some of my music gear and CDs to eat. I was broke, over-whelmed, and at my heaviest. I hated myself. That led to a bout with bulimia. I'd binge eat and then purge until I was empty. I began to feel even worse. I started walking and jogging, trying to reconnect with nature and find peace. I also found this helped with my mental state. My bassist went back to Indiana. I was alone.

That's when I had to learn to survive when I wasn't doing what I wanted to do. My family wouldn't help financially. I had no one to rely on. Then I called Cassandra—my tarot-reading, murder-mystery playwright friend from Indiana. She was in St. Petersburg now. When I told her I was going to pack it up and go back to Indiana, she said, "Hell no, you aren't," and told me to come live with her.

So, I did.

With $75 to my name, I packed my van with my clothes and a guitar and headed to St. Pete. Cassandra, now in her 60s, let me sleep in her little trailer, even sharing her bed. She was my rock—my mentor. We smoked cigarettes, talked for hours, and she poured wisdom into me. I still feel her presence sometimes, like she's a guide.

Within two months, I landed a piercing job at Valhalla Tattoos (now Las Vegas Tattoos) in Ybor City. I also auditioned for a band. Didn't get it, but I stayed motivated. I saved enough to rent a tiny one-bedroom apartment in Tampa. I loved that place. I placed ads to form my own band, and soon, Pretty Machine Gun was born.

At the tattoo shop, I started at the bottom, but after a few months, became the head piercer on weekends and eventually shop manager. This was the early 2000s—Florida's music scene was on fire. I was a little spitfire. I had been growing dreadlocks for years and was a stylish, tattooed, rocker girl. I fit right in. I was making more money than ever, joined a gym, got a personal trainer, and threw myself into working out and music. When I couldn't hit the gym, I'd blast the very first album from the band, Chevelle, and work out at home. (This was the band I named my son after). I was beginning to feel alive again, with luck in my corner. I was also around people who supported me emotionally and believed in what I was doing.

I wasn't dating seriously. I didn't have time with the new band and my full-time job. And truthfully, I hadn't fully gotten over that last relationship in Indiana. He still had a hold on my heart.

I needed help at the shop, so I took on an apprentice. But with weekend shows on the books, she was not equipped to take on the volume our shop was doing. I needed backup. So, I called him up. He moved down immediately. And just like that, we were back in our whirlwind cycle.

It was always the same: good for a month, then chaos. We even got engaged, sent invitations, and called it off. He wanted to change me—how I dressed, how I thought. He wanted a version of me that didn't exist. It couldn't work.

When we finally split again, I was gutted. He moved out of my apartment and into the loft above the tattoo shop. Then he started dating someone from down the street. I saw her all the time. It broke me. I chopped off my dreadlocks right before we split, which was an emotional thing in and of itself—years of growth gone. Symbolic, I guess.

I spiraled into another depression. The only things that kept me going were my band and my job. I devoured books to distract myself and worked out like my life depended on it.

He ended up getting into the Art Institute of Chicago and moved. I was relieved—but not for long. My band broke up shortly after due to creative tension. I felt like life kept kicking me when I was down.

And then, for reasons I still don't fully understand, I followed him to Chicago and gave it another shot. Again.

I don't know if I wanted closure or still believed in us. But we were toxic. I kept going back to someone who wanted me to change and didn't truly love me for me. We had no business being in a relationship. I lasted about four months. I was once again working two jobs and going nowhere. My parents drove up and brought me home.

When I got back to the small town that I spent my entire life trying to escape, I was lost. I was done with piercing, and music had been left to the backburner again. I needed something new. So, I decided to apply to college.

I had to live in Indiana for a year to get in-state tuition at IU, so I worked at a gym (thanks to my dad's connections) and loved it. I eventually got certified as a NASM personal trainer and became an APEX nutrition coach. My eldest sister gave me her old car that wasn't being used. It was old and loud. Trust me when I say you could hear me coming before you even saw me. I was no longer the party girl I had been, at least not to the degree I had been the last time I lived there. I'd go out for drinks with co-workers from the gym, but I hadn't touched drugs in years. I was pretty fit, found some balance, and spent more time with my sister and nephew.

I wasn't dating much—Kokomo didn't have many options. And I still hadn't cut ties with my ex. There was never a clean break. He visited one weekend. We hooked up. I got pregnant.

At first, I didn't tell anyone. I called my friend, Mel, while I was at the drugstore, debating whether to get tampons or a pregnancy test. I chose the test, and it was Positive.

Then, it's as if everything changed overnight. The morning sickness was brutal. I couldn't handle smells I typically could. I eventually lost my job because I couldn't even handle the smell of the gym. I would get nauseated walking in. I even scheduled a termination—but couldn't go through with it. Adoption was also on the table but that didn't feel right either, because I was too judgmental of the people in the packets I would get. I decided to raise my child. I would be 25 by the time I would give birth. I could do this.

I told my family and finally told Jayme. He supported the decision, even though we both knew we'd never work as a couple. My parents were not thrilled but what could they do? By now they knew

I would do what I wanted. I got through my first trimester. I had been living in Indiana for a year and was accepted to IU. I got a job at a girls' home working midnights so I could take care of my baby and still attend college.

I finished my first semester with a 4.0 GPA. I gave birth to my daughter (my now son, Chevelle) that January. I honestly never knew what love really felt like before having this little human. That kind of love is not of this world. Jayme and I tried to make it work for a time, for her sake, but at that point, it was over. We called it quits once and for all and promised to be great parents. He would help me with her, and I continued going to school and working midnights at the girls' home. This was the first time I was able to let this man go. There was real closure. I was finally free.

With help from state assistance, I moved into my own apartment. I was dating a little, but no one measured up. About a year after Chevelle was born, a friend set me up on a blind date. That's when I met C. I was engaged to him—and I broke his heart.

CHAPTER 4

The Big Love Lie

C was a nice, normal guy. No tattoos. Not a partier. He had a healthy sense of self and was steady as a rock in all areas of his life. He lived in Ohio, but his family lived in my town. We met for coffee on our first date. And honestly? I hate to say it, but the physical attraction was never really there. Still, there was something charming about him that made me want to know him better, and we started dating. He'd drive to Indiana. I'd go to Ohio. He took me to shows, wined and dined me. It was easy. Safe. Comfortable.

By then, I had finished my freshman year at IU, was going to school full-time, working full-time, and holding it all together as a single mom. I was doing my best to manage my life, but I was exhausted. I wanted a partner. I wanted support. I wanted a damn break. I wanted security.

Newsflash: being tired and craving stability aren't reasons to get married.

But C had it all together. Nice house. A solid job that he loved. Kind heart. He was generous, loving, and stable. He could provide a real home for me and Chevelle. I was 26 and desperately craving peace. I was convinced—maybe even delusional—that a relationship like this would solve everything.

C and I got serious fast. (Another pattern?) We talked about me moving to Ohio, transferring to Ohio State, and getting married. He'd work. I'd raise Chevelle and finish school. I thought I might work in marketing or PR someday. I didn't know what I was doing, but I thought I did. Then, one night, he made me a cosmopolitan before we went out. I was sipping it, rambling on about something, when he said, "Um, look at your drink."

There was an engagement ring in the bottom of the glass. He had it custom made. And just like that, I was engaged. I said yes. I said I was in love. I said this was my forever.

I lied.

Not maliciously. But I lied to myself. I lied to him. There was no spark. No butterflies. No deep, magnetic pull. I wasn't in love. I was in love with the idea of love. With the idea of safety. Of being chosen. I was in love with the fantasy. I wanted to prove something—to myself, to my parents, to everyone who ever doubted that a tattooed single mom could be worthy of love.

And then there was my dad, who used to say things like, "Who's going to marry a completely tatted-up single mother?" I'd heard it more than once. That my choices made life harder than it needed to be. It was like I was a disappointment. Deep down, his *opinion* caused me to believe my chances were slim. So, when someone "normal" wanted me, I clung to it. C would be the knight in shining armor.

While all this was happening, I was getting back into music—writing again, playing open mics. That's when I met G. And he turned my world inside out.

The spark I never had with C was felt with G immediately. It was undeniable. It was love at first sight, if that's a real thing. That magnetic, "I've known you forever" kind of pull. That spark told me one thing for certain: I could not marry C. Because if you're really in love with someone, you don't have that reaction to someone else. Not like that. At least that's what I told myself.

At first, I tried to ignore it. Laughed it off with friends. Told myself I was being ridiculous. But then, one weekend, a friend invited Chev and me to her lake house—and G was there. His sister was married to my friend's brother. Small world, right?

That weekend changed everything. After one night hanging out with him, I knew I had to call off the engagement. G begged me not to go through with the wedding. He wanted to be with me. He wanted the whole package—me and my child. The feelings were strong, and they were mutual.

But here's the kicker: I'd just moved my things to Ohio the week before. The wedding was planned. Invitations were out. We were supposed to marry in another country and throw a party after. I was in too deep.

And then it all blew up. C found out about G. He'd looked at my MySpace messages and saw everything. He confronted me. I couldn't lie. I had allowed someone else in. Because I was never really in.

Yes, I loved what C did for me. I loved the idea of the life we planned. I did not love him the way he deserved to be loved. And I was selfish for letting it go on as long as I did. I owned that. It wrecked me. Hurting someone who wanted a life with you—someone who loved you—is a pain you don't forget.

I had to make a choice. So, I did.

A friend helped me drive to Ohio with a U-Haul and move everything back out—just a week after I'd moved in. I left the engagement ring. He kept my sacred Taylor guitar. I wanted it back, but he refused. I didn't fight it because I didn't feel like I deserved anything. More guilt. More shame.

I never saw C again.

Years later, I heard he got married and had a family. I wasn't his person. And he wasn't mine. I'm glad he found his path.

It wasn't until I began writing this book when I understood how much those words from my dad shaped the choices I made. When you hear something enough, you start to believe it. I didn't see it then, but I was chasing love from a place of fear—trying to be acceptable, trying to prove I was worthy. Not to myself, but to everyone else. When we make choices from that place, we don't end up with a life that's ours—we end up living someone else's story. This has been the recent wake-up call: love isn't about proving your worth. It's about honoring it. But there would still be many lessons before I would learn this.

Now, let's move on to the next chapter of my life.

CHAPTER 5

The Three-Year Marriage

After the excruciating breakup with C and all the guilt that came with it, I packed my things into storage and moved in with the man who had just flipped my world upside down. He'd recently survived colon cancer and was still recovering from chemo. I loved him deeply. It was sudden, intense, and real. I felt this in my core. I wanted to take care of him and build a life together. Our chemistry was magnetic. Here was this man, a walking miracle with a second chance at life, and I was all in.

I wrote about this relationship in *Unfuckwithable*, but here, I want to go deeper. I was 27 when we got married; he was 44. The age difference didn't faze me. He looked and acted younger, and we both had daughters—his was 14, mine was 3. Both named Bella. We called them Big Bella and Little Bella. (This was before my daughter came out as transgender.)

We needed space for our new blended family and our music, so we bought a beautiful house in Indiana with character, charm, and enough room to build a studio. I was still in school full-time and working full-time. He had a stable job he'd held for nearly two decades. On paper, it all looked right.

But step-parenting was a whole different story. I tried to bond with his daughter, but his parenting style and mine were night and day. He and his ex-wife gave their daughter everything—no boundaries, no limits. If she wanted it, she got it. My upbringing had been the opposite. It didn't sit right with me.

Early on, I noticed red flags. But I couldn't distinguish whether they were true red flags or if I was just uncomfortable. That's the thing—when you're so focused on making something work, it's easy to overlook what your gut is screaming. Maybe you've done this too—quieted your instincts because confronting the truth felt too hard. Ask yourself: *Was I ignoring something real, or just afraid of rocking the boat?*

He would lay with her at night to help her fall asleep—something I figured would fade as she got older. It didn't. I had this gnawing sense that I was suddenly a background character in my own marriage. And deep down, I was already questioning if I'd made a mistake. But I had jumped in headfirst, and now I was committed.

We got married in a small ceremony at our house within six months. On our wedding night, his daughter wanted to sleep over at our place, and he said yes. I had to draw the line.

Our home had become an extension of his ex-wife's—just around the corner. His daughter spent more time with us, and we were constantly in debt trying to keep up with the lifestyle he felt she deserved. He'd fall asleep with her or stay up late watching basketball. I went to bed alone almost every night. Our marriage turned sexless. The loneliness hit hard. I was more alone married than I had ever been single.

I didn't speak up much. When I did, he dismissed me or called me crazy. So, I stopped sharing. I poured myself into parenting, into school, into work. I was spread thin and deeply unhappy. But there were still moments of joy—mostly when music was involved.

We started a band together: *We're Not Mexican.* (Our drummer was Chilean, and everyone assumed he was Mexican—we thought the name was hilarious.) It was rockabilly, surf-inspired, and it was everything to me. He gave me a bass, and though I didn't know it then, it would become one of the greatest gifts of my life.

Playing shows gave me purpose. It was the one place I felt free and capable. We played in Indy, made new friends, and for the first time in a while, I was feeling alive again.

At the same time, I was introduced to the Law of Attraction through a classmate, and then again during my internship in Indianapolis working for my husband's ex brother-in-law and Deborah Farrar. *What the Bleep Do We Know?* blew my mind, and *The Secret* hit home. Everything I was learning about energy, intention, and the power of thought resonated with me in a way nothing else ever had.

I grew up with fire-and-brimstone Christianity, but this was different. This was empowering to me. And it was frowned upon by my husband, who saw it all as nonsense. He was rigid in his thinking as I was expanding mine. We were drifting apart.

His daughter hit high school and began dressing in ways I didn't understand. They let her wear revealing clothes and heavy makeup, and I couldn't wrap my head around it. It all felt like a slow unraveling.

In 2009, I graduated from Indiana University with honors. I was proud. But the divide between us was clear. I was evolving, learning, and reaching. He wasn't. He mocked what I believed in. The loneliness kept expanding. And worst of all, I didn't feel seen.

By the end of that year, we decided to divorce. It was painful but necessary. He wasn't willing to grow, and I couldn't keep shrinking. What hurt the most? Losing the music. The band. The shared creativity. That chapter was closing. But the bass? That stayed with me.

Despite everything, he gave me that. And it changed my life.

CHAPTER 6

Neon Love Life

Because I was working in Indianapolis full time, I needed to move closer to my job. My kiddo's father wanted to keep her there so she would be closer to family, and he was getting married, so he asked if he could take Chevelle on full-time, and I would have her every other weekend and pick her up from school every Wednesday and spend the evening with her. While this was not an easy yes, I knew in my heart that it was best at the time. I was not stable in any way. I didn't have a place to live, I was still trying to figure out what I wanted to do with my career life. There were so many unknowns, and our kiddo needed stability.

I moved out of the home I'd lived in for the last three years that I loved and moved in with my girlfriend and her family in Indianapolis for a short time, while I looked for a place of my own. I stayed with her for a couple of months and was able to find a condo to rent. I moved out of their house and started a new adventure.

New Beginnings

During this time, I had started working for a marketing company, called Rainmakers, and I was also starting my own online marketing company. I was meeting so many different people in the Indy scene. We kept up with our arranged parenting schedule, and things were beginning to have some normalcy.

It was also during this time my spiritual growth was starting to manifest in so many ways. When I look back at the people who were a part of my life at one time, who made such an impact on it, I know I have always been guided by a force outside of myself. I could *feel* it. I was celebrating every single day and living in joy and peace.

My boss at the time, Tony Scelzo, always had a rule for his employees: We were to listen to audiobooks while we were driving that would help us grow as individuals. It was Tony who introduced me to the love of reading self-help. Sure, I'd read plenty of Dr. Phil's *Relationship Rescue* type books in the past, including that one as I was trying to fix Jayme and myself, but that was about as far as it went.

I wanted to dive more into what I had been learning about the Law of Attraction and quantum physics. So now, with all the driving I was doing, I was diving deeper into my spiritual awakening.

My first audiobook was *The Four Agreements* by Miguel Ruiz. I was hearing more things that spoke to my spirit. Enter Dr. Wayne Dyer and Eckhart Tolle, and the dozens of others who have shaped my adult life. I was also in a group coaching program led by my friend, Deseri Garcia, and had been incorporating meditation into my life.

I had already made some connections in the music scene with my old band. I was approached by Sharon Rickson, who played bass in a band called Small Arms Fire. She was heading out to Seattle to volunteer at this camp she had heard of called Girls Rock. Girls Rock is a weeklong, summer day camp for girls ages 8-16, that teaches self-esteem, positive body image, and the power of art through music. The campers would pick their instrument of choice, and we would help create bands for the week. They would name their band, design logos, make zines, write a song, and perform it in front of an always sold-out show by the end of the week. It is basically a DIY clinic for campers interested in music and creation, without the pressures of the opposite sex. We were all about that femme power.

Sharon and I hung out occasionally, got drinks and such. When she got back from her adventure, she called me up, along with Ashley Plummer and Tasha Blackman. We met at Moe and Johnny's, a bar in Broadripple, which would soon become our hangout spot to play pool and drink all the whiskey. We were quite the drinkers back then.

She asked us if we were ready to help bring this nonprofit camp to Indianapolis with her. We all said yes. That's when the idea to start a band with the four of us came about—a band that ended up being my entire life for the next two and a half years. My new obsession. Sharon and I both played bass and guitar, and we both sang, so we would share vocal duties and swap instruments for different songs. Ashley played lead guitar, and Tasha was an amazing drummer. We started getting together that week at Ashley's house, which had the space for us to rehearse. Neon Love Life was born. I had a new creative outlet, and it brought so much joy to my life, which was much needed.

The girls and I were hard at work recruiting our friends and acquaintances in Indianapolis and diving into starting this nonprofit. We put together a board of directors, filed all the paperwork, took a trip to San Francisco to attend the Girls Rock Camp Alliance weekend to learn everything we needed to know to get this camp up and running. This was a place I felt like I fit in. I had new friends, a new band, a new life. I was learning to love my life outside of a marriage I had been drowning in. I had found purpose for the first time in a long time.

I tend to do my best when I'm working toward a goal. I am so blessed in that area to have had many opportunities in my life to throw myself into something. And when I throw myself into something, it's all or nothing with me. This is good and bad because at the time, while I had learned so much from working with my former bosses, I was still so young and didn't understand my own identity. It would take years. My identity was always wrapped up in the things I was *doing*. I felt like I had to do and be something big to make my statement on the world. I had something to prove. And I set out to do that. Still believing I needed to prove my worth.

As the band began, we rehearsed every Monday and Tuesday. We were coming together with ideas and songs, hanging out most nights, and doing everything we could to get Girls Rock Indianapolis launched. We put out press releases, got interviewed, made every connection possible to spread the word. Indianapolis was on board.

Our 501(c)(3) was approved, and we got busy organizing fundraisers and raising money. Our band had its debut show at our first fundraiser. We raised thousands of dollars. We were on top of the world. This was now our life. We all had our day jobs, but by 6 p.m. on any given night, we were all together working on music and growing Girls Rock.

Neon Love Life got signed to an indie label. We were wildly successful during that time. Our album was named #1 by the Indianapolis Star. We put our hearts and souls in it. I didn't really have time for a relationship, so I wasn't dating anyone seriously. This was a time in my life where I felt fulfilled. I was truly living my best life. This was also the time when I had a brief love affair with a married man that I spoke about in my last book.

While I don't want to open old wounds, I need to revisit this. In the midst of all this passion and momentum, there was still a quiet ache inside me—a hunger for something I hadn't yet named. I had a deep craving to be desired. I'm not sure that hunger to be deeply desired ever fully goes away—it just changes shape depending on how seen and valued you feel in your life. I knew at that time I wanted to feel special, chosen, and desired. It's truly difficult when you bond with someone who has a wife and children. I held onto a lot of shame for a long time. But there was a short-term dopamine hit that made it hard to think clearly. I did know one thing though: I would not be the cause of a family breaking up.

We talked and mutually ended it soon after it began. It wasn't right. And we both had too much on the line as leaders in our community. I never wanted anyone to know. My bandmates caught on and weren't happy. I still have deep regrets, and it did come out years later. We both had to make amends. He and his wife worked through it and are still together to this day with a beautiful family. This happened almost 15 years ago.

Despite my lack of judgment during that time, Girls Rock was thriving, and the band was on fire—at least, that's what I believed. Yet another lesson in my life: not all good things are meant to last forever.

CHAPTER 7

When Peace
Meets Paranoia

Enter my next relationship: E was and is very charismatic. We met during the peak of Neon Love Life's success. Our band had been asked to record a cover of a song from Nirvana's *Nevermind*, for its 20-year anniversary, and E was one of the producers on the project. That day in the studio, something clicked. There was an easy chemistry between us—he made me laugh, and we could talk for hours. When we finished recording, he asked me out. I said yes.

He was an amazing producer and musician. He and his twin brother had already been in the music industry for over 20 years, both highly respected and supremely talented.

Because I had been focusing so much on the band and the non-profit, on top of having a roster full of clients with my growing business, I was insanely busy. However, I was getting the itch to be in a relationship. We had so much fun on our first date and decided to continue seeing each other. He had just built a house and asked me to move in with him within two months. It happened quickly, but it seemed like the right thing to do at the time. We had been spending most of our time together anyway, so it all made sense. There I was again, jumping into things quickly—but that's a pattern I hadn't learned to break yet. My motto had become - Go with it. Who knows what will happen?

He was extremely supportive of my band and everything I was doing. But a few months after I moved in, I took one of the biggest hits of my life. My guitarist, Ashley, got accepted to YALE and left the band. I was ready to move on and replace her, but the other members decided to call it quits. This band that I had poured my heart and soul into abruptly ended, and I was in a state of shock. I spent days in bed, once again, spiraling into a deep depression. I had tied my identity so tightly to being in that band, that I actually asked E if he still wanted to be with me if I wasn't in it. Of course, he did—but I had a serious lesson to learn in that moment.

E and I moved on to start a new band together and included his brother. We became a tight-knit family and spent most of our time together. I often wondered if we would ever get married. Something didn't feel quite right, and I wasn't going to push marriage again. I had learned not to rush into something just for the sake of security. E had been married twice before, so we continued living life and doing our thing.

E was and still is a great guy. He wanted to take care of me—and he did. He was driven and successful, spoiled me with shopping trips, and we traveled often. We got along well. He showed up, he supported me in dark moments, and I loved him the best I could. But he also had his own shadows. He was paranoid and often said he trusted no one. I was grounded at this point in my life. I trusted everything and everyone. But the paranoia? It started to seep into our relationship.

I was still part of Girls Rock, volunteering, running my business, and trying to stay mentally and physically healthy. My kiddo spent weekends with us. I was balancing a lot but finding my stride.

Then came another twist. I started playing bass in a different band in Indianapolis called Picture Yes. E had produced their album, and their bassist couldn't make a morning show performance. E asked if I wanted to fill in. It sounded fun—and I loved playing. The guys were great and ended up hiring me long-term. I was writing songs, fronting our newfound band, Kaleidostars, playing in Picture Yes, and everything looked fine from the outside. But something inside our relationship was crumbling: E's self-imposed paranoia.

One day, while I was in the shower, he went through my phone in the downstairs bathroom. He came storming out, furious over a Facebook message from my primary physician asking what I was doing for Christmas. The kicker? The message was from before I even met E. When he realized that, he apologized. Profusely. But it wouldn't be the last time.

I never gave him a reason not to trust me. But he had unresolved guilt from past infidelities and began projecting those fears onto me. That's what projection does—it blurs reality with our worst fears.

Eventually, the accusations and emotional whiplash became unbearable. E began threatening to expose things from my past, particularly the brief affair I had already shared with him. Every argument became a power struggle. I had finally had enough. Anytime I said I was leaving, he would block the door and not let me, saying things would change. One night, in a moment of utter frustration, I threw a bathroom trash can and damaged a door. That wasn't me. That wasn't who I was. And that was my wake-up call.

I had some money saved and rented an apartment. Two of my friends helped me move while E was at work. I blindsided him, but I was done. Too many broken promises to change. Too much emotional exhaustion. We had even been in therapy to work through these things. I didn't want him to know where I was. He begged me to come back, but by then, the love I had for him had turned into a quiet resolve to protect my peace.

Looking back, all these patterns kept emerging. I've always been so loyal. My mom tells me that all the time. I forgive easily. I give people chances. And that loyalty? It can be both my strength and my undoing.

I've talked to so many women about this. We stay. We try. We hope. And then one day—we're just done. The switch flips. And there's no going back.

Projecting

I believe we can only show up in relationships to the extent that we've healed and forgiven ourselves. Projecting our unhealed behavior onto someone else isn't fair—it warps connection.

Let's compare this to peace. If you say you want peace in the world, start by asking: "How am I handling my own peace?"

Are you creating a peaceful environment inside yourself? Or are you projecting fear and chaos outward?

Everything begins and ends with us. Our beliefs shape our reality. E never truly healed from his own choices. His thoughts became his enemies, and they spilled into our life together. And I've done it too. I've watched my mind craft entire false stories—stories that stole my peace.

But I'm learning. I'm learning to slow down. To set boundaries. To honor the flow and honor myself.

Would I have ended up with E if those patterns hadn't existed? Honestly, I don't think so. But I needed that chapter. It led me here. And for that, I'll always be grateful.

CHAPTER 8

Chasing the Sun

After E and I broke up, I found myself spending more and more time with my new band, Picture Yes. My drummer J and I started getting close as friends. He had just gone through a divorce and was staying at his parents' place, where we also rehearsed. I was there often. They had a huge property, and we spent the summer having barbeques and pool parties. The whole band—along with their kids, wives, and girlfriends—became a tight-knit group. They even threw me a birthday party.

J and I leaned on each other for support. One night, down by the river behind his parents' place, we were drinking wine and listening to music. We kissed. It was a little weird, but it felt right. We had become best friends, and our connection was growing. Still, he was seeing other people. I didn't fully trust him with my emotions, even though something deeper was forming between us.

A few weeks later, that something turned into a relationship. Our singer wasn't thrilled but accepted it. We were playing lots of shows and landed a tour with Saving Abel. It would last over a month, so I sublet my apartment, packed a suitcase, and off we went.

Touring the country in a van was freeing. It was my first U.S. tour, and I was buzzing. J and I were getting serious, but I couldn't shake the lingering presence of women he'd dated before me—especially one woman who had recently moved to San Diego. He swore they were just friends, but the texts between them were constant.

When we reached San Diego, he took a call outside the hotel. It was her. He said she was just calling to say she couldn't make the show. I wanted to believe him, but my gut said otherwise. We fought. The tour itself was great, but the red flags were impossible to ignore.

After we got home, J suggested I move in to save money and help with his mom. I was practically living there anyway, so I did. One day, his iPad started lighting up with messages. Curiosity—or intuition—took over. I checked. My heart sank.

The woman from San Diego was pregnant. She wanted money for an abortion. J swore it wasn't his. I still don't know the truth. She ended up getting the abortion. But I was shattered. The timeline confirmed he had been with her and me simultaneously. It was the first time I had been so deeply betrayed as an adult.

I didn't leave. I loved him. We were together every day. He made an effort. Things smoothed out. The texts stopped. But alcohol became our anchor. His mother drank heavily, and so did we—wine, whiskey, bourbon. The partying opened the door to cocaine. It took the edge off—until it didn't.

Our highs were high. We traveled, had fun, and shared so much in common. But our lows were dark—verbal, emotional, and sometimes physical fights. I started losing myself. The spiritual path I'd walked for years felt so far behind me.

In a desperate attempt to reconnect with myself, I picked up *The Power of Now* by Eckhart Tolle. Something began to shift. Then, the call came. Scooter Ward asked if I wanted to join his band, Cold. Without hesitation, I said yes. It felt like divine timing, a spark in the fog.

I didn't feel ready, but I knew this was a gift. I had been disconnected from my source, my intention, my center. The breakup of Neon Love Life had thrown me off-course, but now it felt like the Universe was nudging me back.

Music has always saved me. Cold gave me a new purpose. It helped distract me from the chaos at home. We were still touring with Saving Abel, and I had taken over lead vocals for Picture Yes. J and I even started a new project, naming it Chasing The Sun. It didn't go far, but it was an outlet.

I started meditating again. Journaling. Reading. I wanted to change, to break the cycle. But every time I tried to grow, J accused me of thinking I was "better than him." That's when I knew we were no longer aligned. I wanted to evolve. He wanted to stay where we were.

Reading *The Universe Has Your Back* by Gabrielle Bernstein re-awakened something in me. I remembered that I could choose differently. I didn't have to stay stuck. I began to resent him—and he resented me for my growth and my new opportunity with Cold.

Eventually, I left. I moved back in with my dad. J helped me move, knowing it was over. I turned inward. I got quiet. I got still. And I started to rebuild.

During this time, I posted a photo of all the books I was reading. My old roommate, Hazel Walker, commented: "You're making yourself unfuckwithable." And she was right. That comment sparked something inside me.

The next day, during meditation, the words came: *Write a book. Call it Unfuckwithable. A Guide to Inspired Badassery.* I started writing that day. I was in the ashes of everything, but something new was being born.

Three months later, J and I reconnected. He had been changing. We talked about trying again. He was in LA working on a film, and Scooter had moved to Temecula. I planned to be in California anyway, so J and I agreed to a start fresh out west.

He came back to Indiana. We packed up his car and my life and moved to Venice Beach in the fall of 2016.

At first, things felt new again. I went to Temecula to write with Cold while J worked on his film. When I returned, we moved to Hollywood. I worked on my book, meditated, worked out, and read everything I could get my hands on. I was obsessed with quantum physics and intentions and wanted to include all of this in my book.

We spent the holidays in LA, then I returned to Temecula to go with the guys to record the new Cold album in Arizona. J and I kept in touch, but his insecurity was surfacing again. He was convinced that my success meant I would leave him. I didn't have time for the drama. I had a job to do.

After Arizona, I returned to Temecula to dog-sit. Then back to LA. We moved again—this time to North Hollywood. The kids came for summer, and we had a few beautiful months. We weren't drinking as much while they were there, besides having wine with dinner occasionally. We were focused on family.

It was time for the kids to head back to Indiana, and we had a reunion show planned for Picture Yes. It would be my last. Once the band arrived, the drinking started again and the drugs. I hated who J became when he was drunk—mean, unpredictable. At the show, I was embarrassed because everyone was drunk onstage. It was sloppy. This wasn't who I was anymore. I was now part of Cold. I needed to rise.

That night, at our apartment, everything imploded. In front of others, J ripped my favorite hat off my head, threw it over the balcony, and dumped a bottle of Benadryl on my head. That was my line. I called Scooter. He and his wife offered me a place to stay.

I packed up my Mini Cooper and left.

J had supported me financially. He took care of us, and we shared amazing experiences. But I had stayed out of obligation. Because I thought I owed him. But no more.

It was time to choose myself.

I was ready to stop running from my peace and start chasing the light within me.

Reclaiming Myself

There's something liberating about finally choosing yourself—not from a place of anger, but from a place of truth. I didn't leave because I hated him. I left because I had finally remembered who I was.

And once you remember, you can't forget again. Not fully. Not for long.

That was the beginning of my rise back to alignment—with music, with spirit, with self-worth.

I wasn't chasing the sun anymore. I was becoming it.

The Long Goodbye

Sometimes, it's not the first red flag that makes us leave. Or the second. Or even the tenth.

We stay because we remember the good times. Because we've invested so much.

Because we think maybe, just maybe, this time they'll finally see us the way we see them.

We stay because leaving means facing the unknown—and for many of us, familiar pain feels safer than uncertain peace.

I stayed far longer than I should have—not just with J, but in so many spaces, with so many people who couldn't meet me where I was headed. This will not be the last time I find my myself here. I stayed because I wanted to believe.

In the good.
In the potential.
In love.

And while that belief is beautiful, it can also keep us stuck in cycles we outgrew long ago.

The truth is, most of us don't leave the moment it hurts—we leave the moment we finally believe we're worth more than the hurt.

I wasn't weak for staying. I was human.

But I became powerful when I finally chose myself.

CHAPTER 9

When Love Is
a Double Life

That next week, I got settled into Temecula. Because I hadn't worked in a while, and I didn't know anyone in the area, I knew my first order of business was to find a job. I didn't have a lot of bills, just some small things here and there. My car had been paid off for years. I figured the best way to meet people and get to know the city was to work in the service industry. So, I went for the best place I could in Old Town—The Goat and Vine. I don't know how I managed to land that coveted spot, but somehow, I did. And honestly, that job was exactly what I needed at that time. I ended up meeting one of my best friends, Brandy, who also worked there. She is still like a sister to me.

Life started feeling full again. I was meeting people, making friends, working hard, and loving it. I also started helping with a podcast in San Diego called *The Dusty Futon* with my friends, Kim and Jon Campos. I reconnected with my friend, Shana, from Gainesville so I was going to Newport Beach often to hang out with her. I was happy, I had a social life, I was rehearsing nonstop because Cold was slated to tour soon. My book moved to the back burner. I was dating casually, but no one really stuck out or felt like a future.

Eventually, Scooter and his wife moved out of the house, and I moved in with a family who rented me a room in their huge home. I lived there for a year. Around that time, Goat and Vine started scaling back staff, and I was let go. I ended up getting a bartending and serving job in Fallbrook and made even more friends. I was going out a lot with coworkers after shifts, and alcohol and drugs were becoming more and more a part of my normal life. But I was having a blast.

One night, a guy came into the restaurant and sat at the bar while I was working. He was handsome, a little dorky, but flirty and sweet. I had no idea he would end up breaking my heart. Here is that story.

I moved to Fallbrook to be closer to work and rented out a basement from new friends. It was a perfect short-term setup. I started dating B while still living in Temecula but saw him more once I moved, since he lived in Fallbrook too. He worked as a supervisor for an energy company, on long shifts in Alhambra. When he wasn't with his two kids, he was with me. We had undeniable chemistry, and I loved that he wasn't in the music industry. It felt simple.

About six months in, I had no idea he was seeing someone else. We had talked about being exclusive but hadn't officially defined things. After all, I didn't want to push anything and was playing it cool. I would hashtag his name in posts since he didn't have social media. So, when a stranger commented on one of our photos asking me to check my DM requests, I was stunned.

It happened while I was camping with another one of my best friends, Noel, who loved B and thought we were a great couple. Everyone did. I checked my messages and found one from a woman claiming he had been living a double life. He stayed with her when he wasn't with me. They'd been on and off for years. Shock, sadness, anger—all of it hit me at once. I replayed everything in my head: the phone always being off, the secretive texting. It was all there, and I had ignored it, because I was trying to trust and not be in my head over things that had happened in my past.

I sent B a screenshot of this message, and he immediately called. He confessed. He said she was the reason his marriage ended. They'd been off and on for over a decade. He told me he was trying to get out, that he loved me, and he'd understand if I never wanted to see him again.

I cried all night. Noel helped me through it. But by the next day, I was making excuses. We always had fun. We weren't "official." I still wanted to see him. It sounds insane now, but I didn't have the self-respect then to walk away. I still wanted to be *chosen*.

So, I stayed. A few weeks later, we had a serious talk and committed to a relationship. He introduced me to his family. I spent time with his kids. I felt like it was finally happening, that he could be the *one*. It felt good—for a while.

Then one night at a bar, he got a text. A topless photo from *her*, with a message about seeing him soon. I lost it. I took his phone and threw it across the bar. He left me there. No car, no ride, no goodbye. Just gone. My roommate Chet came and picked me up. I was too angry to cry.

But it wasn't over. B came back, apologized, begged for another chance. And I let him in. Again. Chet hated him. He once came to the house and Chet kicked him out. I should have too.

I was about to go on tour. Chet and Erin were selling the house, so I moved into a friend's place nearby. I was going to be gone for three months. B even flew out to Atlanta to see me on tour. He stayed for a few shows. It was sweet, but I was annoyed. He didn't fit in. He didn't get the lifestyle, and he didn't fit the vibe. And being on tour is a *vibe*.

After he left, and she had seen that he had traveled to see me, *she* made an Instagram account full of photos of her and B just for me to see. I stopped taking his calls. I was done. For a bit.

Back in Fallbrook post tour, B reached out again. He'd bought a house in Temecula. Wanted to take me out. Show me the house. And again, the cycle began. We had so much fun. The chemistry was fire. But now I know: Chemistry isn't enough. As Matthew Hussey says, "Attention is not intention."

We kept seeing each other. Spent the holidays together. I stopped asking questions. I didn't want answers. I just wanted the good parts.

Then came the pandemic. I moved in with my best friend Tricia and her fiancé three days after the shutdown. Touring was canceled. My old roommates were partying, everyone was coming over, and I didn't feel safe. Tricia had a farm, and I moved in. It was perfect.

During the six months I stayed there before moving back to LA, B and I were still seeing each other. He even came to visit once I moved. By then, it had been two years of this cycle. But it never ended with a bang. It just fizzled. No closure. No official goodbye.

That was the last time I saw him. The trust had been shattered. I had changed. I wanted more—to be chosen, fully. And I was finally learning to choose myself. At least for now in this moment. I would not be completely done with liars and cheaters quite yet. Thankfully, I was able to spot them much quicker. We'll get to that.

The Inner Battle with Betrayal

It saddens my soul when look at why I stayed. I really did love him. We don't just stay for love—we stay for the *hope* that the lies were temporary. That the truth was misunderstood. That what we felt was real, even if their actions said otherwise.

But being lied to doesn't just break your heart—it messes with your sense of reality. You start questioning your instincts, your memory, your worth. You wonder how someone who claimed to care for you could look you in the eyes and hide entire parts of their life.

That kind of betrayal lingers.

Every lie I uncovered made me lose a piece of myself. Not just because he deceived me—but because I kept making space for it. I kept convincing myself that love required sacrifice. That maybe honesty was optional if the connection was strong enough.

But it's not. Love without honesty isn't love. It's performance. It's possession. It's pretending. I've even been on the lying part of it, as you'll soon see. Not to the same extent. But lies are lies. And they cause serious damage.

But with B, I didn't just walk away from him—I walked away from every version of me that accepted less than the truth. And in doing so, I finally started writing a story that felt honest. One where I chose *me*—without apology, without exceptions, and without his lies.

CHAPTER 10

Frogs Don't Turn into Princes

The following year, I was back to living my best life—or so I thought. I was partying with my friends, hungover most days, but still working out, drinking all the water, and eating clean. There was a part of me that knew I was destroying myself, but I didn't care. I felt free. Creative. Wild. I also knew I'd be leaving soon for tour, and when that happens, I usually slow down and get laser-focused on being in top shape for stage.

An old friend I'd met at SXSW hit me up when he saw I was living in LA. We'll call him X. He'd moved here too and asked if he could take me out. I hadn't seen him in eight years. He worked at a comedy club in Hollywood and invited me to a show. I rallied one of my girlfriends—despite my hangover—and we went.

We hugged. It was good to see him. He treated us like VIPs that night—great seats, anything we wanted. Before I left, he asked to see me again. I said yes.

It's funny how quickly your brain can spiral when someone shows interest. *"Could this be the one?"* I wondered.

We went on a date a few nights later. He came to pick me up, and his car was disgusting—inside and out. It was like a rolling dumpster. He looked like he'd had a couple glasses of wine already. I gave him shit about the car but tried to chill and enjoy the night.

He took me to Sugar Fish, his favorite sushi spot in LA. We drank a few bottles of wine and ordered basically everything. It was fun and flirty. We talked about dating apps. Tinder was huge at the time. I'd never used them—too weird with my career, and besides, I wanted to meet people naturally. He said the same. *"Not my thing,"* he told me. Just first-date chatter, right?

He came over for a bit afterward, then left so I could sleep. Over the next few weeks, we started hanging out more. But there were red flags everywhere. His house was always a mess. He was messy. That damn car was still a wreck. And I was pretty sure he was a raging alcoholic. But I wasn't looking for anything serious, and I was leaving for tour in less than a month. So, I stayed casual.

And yet—this man started talking about taking me to Scotland, traveling with me, even moving in together. Love bombing much? I get it. I'm cool, but this was a bit aggressive. Still, I soaked up the attention. It had been missing from my life.

The final time I hung out with him, he had work colleagues in town and wanted me to join them for a night out in Hollywood. Side note: he was always talking about how much money he had. It never impressed me. I've dated people with money—it means nothing to me. Kindness and honesty? That's the real currency. I make my own money. Okay, back to the story.

We Ubered to a restaurant before meeting his friends. When we got there, I realized I'd left my glasses in the car. I can barely see without them, so he handed me his phone to call the driver. I pulled down on the screen to search for the Uber app, and there it was— Tinder. His most-used app.

I was stunned. I didn't let it show. This man had lied to me for weeks, saying he wasn't on any dating apps. Telling me he was falling in love with me. I called the Uber, stayed calm, and decided to go through the evening as planned, though my heart was beating out of my chest. We met his colleagues at the club, and I drank myself into a state where I just didn't care.

Back at his place, we were watching TV. He passed out, phone open, because the remote was on it. Then came the texts—from his ex. "I love you." "I miss you." "Can't live without you." All from him. He had been seeing her the whole time too.

I called an Uber and left without waking him.

A few days later, I found out more. He'd told me he couldn't attend my going-away party because he had to fly to New York to work on a song for a Pixar film. Okay, sure. But he had logged into his email on my computer. I was angry enough to do some digging.

Turns out, he wasn't going to New York. He was flying another woman in from Chicago—a *different* woman, not his ex. I saw her flight confirmation in his inbox. He was also telling her he loved her. The lies were endless.

I blocked him everywhere and went on a bender with my friends. I was pissed.

What hit me hardest wasn't the guy—I didn't even like him that much. It was the *lies*. I would've been fine with the truth. I wasn't asking for a relationship. I just didn't understand why he lied at all. What was he trying to gain?

Somehow, I connected with the girl from Chicago. We talked on the phone for two hours. She told me he had tried to get her pregnant and had *actually* gotten someone else pregnant. She said during her trip to LA, he was weird and didn't want to go out. Now she understood why—my party was that weekend. He couldn't risk being seen with her.

My ego was bruised, but my intuition had been right all along. The Universe protected me.

I packed my bags. It was time to leave LA for a bit.

My friend, Echo picked me up in her Mercedes Sprinter van, and we hit the road to Indiana. A ten-day trip across the country. I left it all behind. In the rearview. I'd been drinking too much. I needed to reset. My birthday was coming up, and I promised myself that after that day, I'd clean things up—eat better, train harder, rehearse. Tour started in two months.

Echo and I had one of the best adventures of my life. We laughed. We cried. We vented. We made memories. From Zion National Park, hot springs in Colorado, dinners with friends, to nights at the Ritz in St. Louis making new friends, we had a blast. We landed in Indiana just in time for my friend's birthday. Everything felt magical.

I felt deeply blessed—by the Universe, by friendship, by this strange little detour that became a healing journey.

Once my birthday hit, it was game on. Two months of intense focus. I headed to Pennsylvania for pre-production with the band. We were ready.

When Someone Lies, Believe Them

It's not always the heartbreak that hurts the most. Sometimes, it's the *insult* of being lied to. Of someone thinking so little of your intelligence, your worth, or your honesty, that they feed you bullshit when you never even asked for the truth to be sugar-coated.

I wasn't devastated because I loved him—I didn't. I was devastated because I trusted him, and he didn't deserve it. And maybe even more than that, I was angry with myself for brushing off the signs I *clearly saw.*

There's a kind of grief that comes when you realize you gave someone the benefit of the doubt, and they just saw it as a free pass.

So, here's what I've learned from both B and X: When someone lies to you, don't make excuses for them. Don't minimize it. Don't romanticize their potential. Believe them. Believe what they show you. Believe the contradiction. Believe the silence.

Because frogs don't turn into princes. They just stay frogs. And sometimes, they croak the loudest when you're finally walking away.

And to the guys who lie to women they're dating: *Sir, I assure you, I'm not the IRS. You don't have to lie to me.*

CHAPTER 11

Narcissism 101 — The BIG Red Flag Chapter

B eing a public figure, I have many people in my online world. This is where my next relationship would come into play—at a time when, despite all the healing work I'd done, there was still a soft spot in me that craved connection. What unfolded was the last thing I expected. And the red flags weren't subtle—they were practically neon. But I was still wearing those rose-colored glasses until they finally cracked.

We started off as Facebook friends. We had a mutual friend—someone I admired and respected in the music industry. That connection gave me a false sense of security. I thought, *"Hey, if this guy is friends with him, he must be an alright human."* What I didn't realize at the time was that this seemingly harmless beginning would spiral into one of the most eye-opening, relationships of my life—and that the craving for connection would blind me to the warning signs I'd learned to spot in others, but still struggled to recognize in real time. And it's a story we hear all the time.

D was extremely attractive. We were both in our 40s. He had a girlfriend during the time we became friends (of course he did—because he's the kind of guy who always has someone on the line). He never really "flirted" flirted with me during this time, which I actually appreciated. When I flirted with him a bit in the beginning, he let me know he was in a relationship. Respect, I thought. There's also the fact that I live in Los Angeles, and he was in New Jersey, right outside NYC. So, there was that whole distance thing.

I hadn't been in a committed relationship going on five years. While I had my moments of being in love with B, he was never *really* my boyfriend.

Because I tour so much, and I'm in a band where I'm typically the only female on the road, I've come to accept that my lifestyle isn't exactly conventional or easy for most to understand. It takes a certain kind of person to be okay with the long stretches of absence, the constant travel, and the reality that I often exist in my own orbit. That said, I've always had a solid support system—my family, my bandmates, and my incredible friends in Southern California and across the country. I feel fulfilled on my own as a writer, a creator, and a human who genuinely loves life. But even with all of that, I still held space in my heart for a relationship—one that felt right. Because let's be real—who doesn't want to find their person, someone who gets it and rides the wave alongside you??

Our online friendship overlapped with the 2020 election, during which I was extremely vocal. D often came to my defense on social media when people disagreed with me politically. I didn't slam people's opinions or call names—D did that for me. At first, I found it thoughtful. *"Look at this guy, defending me so passionately!"* But it wasn't just passion—it was intensity laced with hostility. When he started getting aggressive in my comment sections, I had to private message him and ask him not to call people names. Let's call that Red Flag Number One: that fire wasn't passion—it was volatility in disguise.

My band kicked off our 2021 fall tour on the east coast. On the second night, we landed in northern New Jersey. It was a full moon on that September night, and I posted a story. D immediately hit me up on Instagram and asked where I was. Turns out, I was ten minutes away. I had the next night off, so I sent him my number. He texted me two minutes later and asked if I wanted to grab a bite. I said yes. I did ask my drummer to join us though, because I'm not stupid.

The next evening, he showed up at the tour bus, and the three of us went for tacos. He was sexy, funny, charming, well-dressed, and worked in sales. He drove a nice car—not a requirement for dating me, but it showed he was seemingly able to manage his life. We shared our first kiss that night. He came to the show the next evening. After, everyone including D was hanging out on the tour bus, laughing, drinking, and having a great time. We made plans to go to Costa Rica in February once the tour and holidays were over.

Fast, right? I justified it by saying, *"I'm an adventurer."* I was already planning a solo Costa Rica trip, so when I asked half-jokingly if he wanted to join me, and he said yes, I figured why not? He seemed spontaneous, like me. And maybe a master manipulator too—I'd soon find out. Plus, I'm a firm believer that you can learn about someone pretty quickly when you travel with them. And I wanted to get to know this human because I was very attracted to him.

From there, we dove in. Facetiming constantly, making plans, getting caught up in the newness of it all. When he visited again a couple weeks later, we stayed in an Airbnb, drank wine, and he brought all kinds of gifts (he even brought presents for my bandmates). He told me that night that he was in love with me.

That was fast. I mean, this person doesn't even really *know* me. I had caught onto X's love bombing, but I wasn't really into X. I was into this guy, so naturally, I overlooked it. I took it as genuine.

(I'm rolling my eyes so hard over here.) In hindsight, it was another red flag I dressed up as romantic intensity. Because when you *want* something to work, you'll find ways to excuse behavior that looks suspiciously familiar.

Things got weirder in these 24 hours. During dinner with my bandmates the next evening, as the waitress struggled to understand my wine order, D mumbled under his breath, but loud enough for the entire table to hear it, *"dumb cunt."* I laughed nervously, but I was horrified. Everyone else was horrified. After he left, and I was confronted by my bandmates that they didn't think he was someone I should be dating, I explained it away as him being sarcastic or joking, but that was Red Flag Number Two. Actually, maybe Red Flag Number Three. I even sent the badass attorney friend of my bandmate who had also been at that dinner, flowers the next day to apologize on his behalf because they were so mortified. I also know how much my bandmates care about me, so I told myself they were being overprotective, and they didn't know the person I had been spending time with as well as I did. I was fooling myself.

Thanksgiving came, and I spent it with D and his family because I was in the area with a few days off. This was also my first time going to his home that he shared with his teenage son, and I was excited to see what I could possibly be getting myself into if things were to progress. That night seemed normal. It felt like we were creating something real.

My tour wrapped up, so that first week of December, I went back to his place for a visit. Right away, I started to see how he interacted with people. More red flags came. He was aggressive on the road, drove too fast, screamed at other drivers, and I didn't feel safe. I was not okay with how he would speak to his son, either. He would call him names and bullied him. As I'm typing this out right now, I can't believe I not only stayed, but I would soon move across the country.

But there's always that hindsight of what we *"could have"* or *"should have"* done.

After our visit, I flew to Chicago to spend time with my friends and see a band that we love, and then back to Indiana to spend time with my son. So far, no REAL drama between us; I ignored the things that made me wonder and kept looking for the good. We decided he would fly to Indiana to meet my kid and my family for the holiday.

Because I was staying at my mom's, I rented an Airbnb in Indianapolis so we could all have our own space for the week. He and his son flew in on Christmas Day. We headed to my mom's the day after to celebrate. That week, we spent time with my family, my kiddo, and the kids got along great. He was charming with my family, and everyone seemed to approve of him. Things seemed good, except for him snapping at me for asking if he wanted to stop and get cigarettes in front of his son. Which was weird because we all knew he smoked. Hell, he smoked in this bedroom bathroom. It wasn't something he hid. I didn't understand. I just apologized and dropped it, despite how it made me feel.

During this trip, we had a real discussion about me packing up my LA place in January and moving in with him. I was on a month-to-month lease then, and we figured why spend money on two places? Besides, I had a tour coming up in a couple of months, and we wanted to spend as much time as possible with one another. I was for it, even though I was ignoring everything in me saying something was off.

I left mid-January for LA, spent two weeks there with my friends, packed my apartment, and the movers came and got my things. It would take a few weeks for my things to get across the country, so I decided to fly back to Jersey because there was a show I wanted to attend. (I'm always traveling for music.) I invited a friend to join D and me on the drive to Pennsylvania to see my bandmates' other band. D was driving, and he was driving like an asshole, despite me letting him know I took issue with that. The entire time he went too fast, weaving in and out of traffic and was scaring me. When I asked him to slow down, he snapped at me in front of my friend. D knew I have had a fear of car accidents since I was little. It's a serious thing for me. One straw that broke the camel's back in my last long-term relationship was my ex's blatant disrespect for driving at a normal speed. So, this was happening, and I was pissed. I think it was at that moment that my respect for him started to decline. However, my things were currently being moved across the country, so I had to ride this out. We went to the show. He drove just as terribly on the way home, and he was rude to my friend. We went home. *Red flags.*

When the movers finally gave me a date for the arrival of my things, I flew to the Midwest to meet them because I would not be moving all my belongings yet, so they went into a storage unit close to my mom's house. I rented a vehicle on February 14th to move only the items I needed to get me through the next month and through the tour. I drove 12 hours to New Jersey.

The effort I put in to get there—packing, driving 12 hours, juggling my schedule—none of it was acknowledged. It was Valentine's Day. He met me outside the apartment, looked at my car full of belongings, and the first words out of his mouth were: *"What are we going to do with all this shit?"* No *"Happy Valentine's Day."* No *"How was your drive?"* No flowers, no hug, no warm welcome. Nothing. That was when I knew the honeymoon phase was officially over. He didn't feel like he had to win me over anymore—because I had already moved across the country. Red flag, flaming red. I cried myself to sleep that night.

The Costa Rica trip was the following week, and what was supposed to be a magical escape turned out to be a nightmare. He berated the rental car clerk over a $500 credit card hold. It was so bad that they refused to rent to him but would thankfully rent to me. I apologized profusely for his behavior while he went to "cool off," by having a cigarette and told the clerk he was "exhausted" from the long day of travel. The remainder of the trip was eye-opening. He wore headphones by the pool, air-drummed like he was Bonham, chain-smoked constantly, spent most of the time on his phone, and barely engaged with me. It was like traveling with a self-absorbed teenager. I ended up paying for the rental car, and he didn't even reimburse me, though he said he would.

We flew back to his place on the east coast, and I was off to LA the next day to see Manchester Orchestra with my Chicago friends who were also flying in for the show. Another friend, who would end up being my next relationship, joined us for dinner, but we'll get to that later.

I was basically off the grid because I was spending time with my friends and trying to shake off the emotional residue from the week before. I had planned on staying at my best friend's apartment, and as luck would have it, some of our other friends from the building came by unexpectedly. We ended up catching up late into the night. It was one of those spontaneous, healing evenings—the kind that brings you back to life. I wasn't about to "check in" with my boyfriend at 5am his time. I'm an adult, I was with people who know and love me, and frankly, I respect boundaries and sleep schedules. What he expected was unreasonable—it was control, disguised as concern.

The following morning there were a fury of unfriendly texts. I apologized for not texting the night before and told him he was right and that I should have been more considerate. But rather than letting it go at that, he continued to berate me the entire time I was there. Also, knowing I was there to see my favorite band, he made my whole day leading up to it completely miserable. It jolted my focus, and now I was getting his controlling behavior aimed at me.

Red flag! Red flag! Red flag! Honestly, had I not moved, I never would have spoken to him again.

I flew back to the east coast and had to start prepping for the tour. I spent most of my time in our then bedroom rehearsing and ensuring I had all the songs down for the set we were about to embark on for two and a half months. I had two weeks until I was heading to Pennsylvania for rehearsal. It was a reasonably calm two weeks, because I spent nearly all my time rehearsing and by myself. I was also pouring candles for the tour, so I stayed busy. I wanted to be anywhere but there.

He drove me to the studio where we rehearsed with my things. We said our goodbyes; then it was all band. Music is my happy place. Touring is something I absolutely love to do. I love meeting fans and being with my band family. I love being a part of something so extraordinary. D would always tear our fans down. He would talk so much shit about everyone for no reason to make himself feel superior. Then, he started tearing down MY personal friends, which is entirely unacceptable. *(Red flag, anyone?)* So many things were beginning to bother me. I'd lost all respect. I was really starting to see his energy and his insecurities. But again, here I was and had moved across the country to see if this was something that would work. But for now, I got a break. I was back to doing what I loved.

D and I Facetimed every day during pre-production for the tour. I hadn't really hit a *breaking* point at this time, though I was becoming very numb. I figured I'd deal with it when the time came, and it wasn't right then.

The band hit the road with gusto. We had a show on the east coast in Jersey about a week or two in. He brought all his friends to the show, and it started out as a great night. But unfortunately, this was the night our relationship *really* started to unravel. (I mean, technically, it began to unravel when he yelled at me for asking him to drive like a normal person; however, this is where it took a definitive spiral.)

I got a little buzzed after the show because I knew I was going to be at our apartment that night, and we were going to have a cookout the next day. Some of our road crew were up in the apartment after the show, and I wanted to walk the dog. D was so rude to me, that my guitar tech refused to come back up to the apartment the next day. He also responded rudely to one of my friend's texts, who was going to come up the next day for the cookout. My friend, rather than confronting D, just deleted him on all social media. Once D realized this fact, he became so enraged, and he demanded I delete him from MY social media. This is a guy I've known for close to a decade. *More red flags.* That controlling, manipulative bullshit was coming to the surface in a serious way. I left with my band the next night, and I was already over it. I was just so grateful I was going to be gone for a while. I would deal with it after the tour was over.

That tour did not go well in terms of the two of us. I wanted nothing to do with him. He wanted to know who I was with and what I was doing the entire time. Some nights, I flat out refused to call him. One of my friends that we always see on tour had come to one of our shows. She knows me very well. I walked out to see her and spend time with her and the first words out of her mouth were, "What is going on? This is not the loving, happy Lindsay I know." She knew nothing of the story.

My energy was being depleted and it was OBVIOUS. I was done. However, he had already booked a trip to see us in LA. I told him not to come. He came anyway. He begged me to stay with him and not give up on us so quickly. In that moment, because he was crying literal tears, and I'm not a fan of confrontation or hurting people, the soft spot in me decided I'd see what would happen when I got back, rather than moving out immediately, as I had planned. I knew bits about his past and some of the unresolved trauma from how he grew up and was raised. I felt like if he could get help, maybe it was salvageable. But deep down I knew it wasn't.

Once I was home from the tour, I lasted less than six weeks. And for probably four of those weeks, I was letting him know it wasn't working for me. For weeks, I told him I wasn't happy. For weeks, I asked him to start reading and evolving. And for weeks, he ignored my requests, and spent all his time on social media and chain smoking outside. I had finally had enough.

I started writing this part of the book the night I rented a moving truck. The next day, I continued to add to this story... in between him coming in to scream at me about how he behaved because of MY BEHAVIOR. The blame game was never ending. I had come to peace with my decision to leave because I had been meditating on it for weeks. I also had friends in my corner giving me strength. There was definitely a sense of relief once I made the decision. A relief that in 48 hours, I would be moving my things and would no longer be walking on eggshells. I wouldn't have to deal with his blame or anger anymore.

The next day, all hell broke loose when I told him I was leaving. I was actually scared. He became so angry and irrational that he tried to blackmail me into staying. I had been vulnerable enough to trust him with a glimpse into my past, and he used it as ammunition. All I could do was lock myself in the bathroom while my voice memo app recorded him screaming at me, making threats against me, calling me terrible names, spewing lies, and talking mad shit. It gives me anxiety just thinking about it. It took seven weeks for me to share my story when I first wrote about this on a public forum.

During all this yelling and emotional abuse, I was holding onto a rose quartz a friend had gifted me, and I was singing the Highly Suspect version of "Send me an Angel" in my head, almost as a praying mantra over and over again. Every time I would try to pack, he'd throw my things across the room. He was not ready to let me leave. Because I had locked myself in the bathroom just to work my normal day job, my boss had HAD it. She called me at 10:30pm and said, *"Pack a bag, my husband and I are coming to get you, this is abuse, and I'm not allowing it."*

The police escorted me out safely and took note of my belongings, because he had threatened to destroy them or keep them during his screaming fits. The Universe heard me that night and literally sent me an angel. Many angels for that matter. Another dear friend went with me to pick up the moving truck, and we got my things three days after I left him. My Mom told me I could stay with her while I planned my voyage back to the west coast, because the west was truly home for me.

The post-traumatic stress I suffered was real, even though he was never physically violent. But the anxiety I would get as I was trying to share my story is a REAL thing. It took me a very long time to heal from it. I can't imagine how many women are dealing with these same experiences.

D lost his girlfriend and his dog from cancer within four days of each other. He had a breakdown. I wanted to think D was not a bad person. He is who he is. I always had hope that he would find his way. I have no idea if he has. He spent months still contacting me telling me he was changing and reading books and seeing a therapist for his anger issues.

He made it clear that he wanted to reconcile with me. But it was way too late. I thought at the time, maybe I was there to wake him up and the Universe gave me that responsibility because I could handle it. I held so much hurt, anger, and resentment in my heart and soul, that it took a physical toll on my body. I had never been so grateful to get away from someone as I had from him.

He continued to try to contact me for months after I had blocked him. He created a new email account to reach me. Sent flowers to my mom. Threatened my friends and bandmates and even threatened the man who I'd find myself in a relationship with next. It was terrifying. But I made it out. And through all of that, something beautiful happened—I reconnected with my mom. We healed our relationship. She became my best friend. I would've never imagined that. That alone made it all worth it.

Here's what I've learned:

Again, if someone shows you who they are, believe them. If they show you red flag after red flag, don't convince yourself you're special or exempt. Don't move across the country for someone you barely know. Don't override your gut. And most importantly, never forget:

> *"What is meant for you will not pass you by.*
> *And you can't lose anything that is good for you."*
> —Dr. Wayne Dyer

Even the worst relationships can bring clarity, growth, and unexpected gifts.

But next time… I'll run faster.

CHAPTER 12

The Edge of
Something Real

A little preface:
I feel like I have been going through a breakup with the same person for the better part of two and a half years. The constant back and forth, the ups and downs, and the inability to let go out of fear—while also evolving into a better human—have made this the most transformative relationship of my life. I lost so many nights of sleep and cried too many times to count. The fact that I continually pushed for something, despite all the signs that he was not the person for me, had my head spinning by the last time around. But this would be the relationship that opened my eyes.

Before I dive into this story, I need to share a little Universal truth: When you ask God, the Universe, Source Energy, Zeus, or whoever you pray to—or have quiet conversations with—for something new to enter your life, that aligns with who you truly are and what you desire, don't be surprised when the old starts to crumble. It's wild to witness. I was finally seeing my patterns that needed to be broken. And even though I did everything I could to make it work, it just would not.

I had been writing this chapter for a while, never quite knowing how it would turn out.

He had been my mirror for the last two and a half years. When we finally called it quits, I wasn't just disappointed—I was frustrated with myself for letting him back in again. A relationship cannot survive when your needs are consistently unmet. It doesn't matter how much love you feel or how tightly you cling to the fantasy you've built. People can only love you to the extent that they are capable of. My needs were never a priority. I spent so much time stuffing them down. The person I betrayed most was myself.

By now, I know I am a lover. I know who I am, what my values are, and what I stand for. I love to nurture. I'm a giver. And I truly did love M. I gave it everything I had. But I'd been fighting a battle of dreams versus reality for far too long.

This was a love I had to let go of to reclaim what I had so easily handed over, even after all I had learned from all the other ones. For a year, I waited for reciprocity that only came once I finally gave up. This relationship changed me. It shook me to my core. It awakened strength I didn't know I had and forced me to finally stand in the truth.

We make choices during high-anxiety moments, and if you're anything like me, we question those choices after. So much history, good and bad, was created in our time together. We had a cycle: one of us wouldn't get our needs met. I would stay quiet, terrified of "rocking the boat." We'd break up. I'd get blamed. I'd beg him to come back. Then we'd get back together, and I'd spend days unable to eat or sleep, convinced I was the problem. And maybe, sometimes, I was. But I wasn't the only one.

I had dreamed of marrying this man for five years. The irony? I didn't even know him when I made up that dream. Maybe it was a seed my bestie, Tricia, had planted. I know she just wanted to see me happy after everything I had been through.

But even when we used to hang out early on, years before our relationship, and despite what my friend had said, which we will get to, I always had this voice in the back of my head saying he was "the one." He had a calming presence. He wasn't loud or attention-seeking like everyone I had dated before. He was different. Something in me whispered, *"This is it."*

I clung to that feeling even when the reality gave me nothing but anxiety and sadness. He had his own stuff, and on top of it, he "wasn't sure about me." I guess he had his own red flags about me.

Still, I visualized our life together. I would meditate and picture us dancing, laughing, living an incredible life—married, with a home and an amazing connection. Cooking together. Making out on countertops. Meditating together—even though I had no clue what his beliefs were. Hiking, traveling, building a life full of love and growth. The dream was vivid. But it was far from the reality I stepped into. And yet I held onto it like my life depended on it.

Once I ended things with D, I focused entirely on M. He had been in a relationship for a couple of years, and we were still friends—though I knew I could fall in love with him. We'd talk on the phone for hours while I was preparing to move back to LA. I asked the Universe for a sign, like Gabby Bernstein talks about in *Super Attractor.* I chose an owl. *"If this is right, show me owls."* And wouldn't you know it, owls started appearing everywhere. Maybe I was looking for them. Maybe not. But to me, it felt like a yes. Sometimes, yes for now isn't a yes forever.

I know we sometimes see what we want to see. But I saw signs, they were there. I paid attention. Maybe he wasn't meant to stay, but I believed we were forever—even though I still had so much healing and growing to do.

Let's go back to the beginning...

I met M in the fall of 2019. I was living in Fallbrook, CA at the time and had just gotten home from my fall tour with Cold. I was casually playing card games with my friend, Claire, and drinking all the red wine, when I get a call from my best friend, telling me I needed to go to her house immediately because she wanted to introduce me to the man I was going to marry.

Out of pure curiosity—because my bestie has a witchy sense about her—my friend and I rallied and went over to her house, which was only a couple of miles away. When I saw him, I felt this warmth. I was being flirtatious as we talked about the music industry—he was part of it too—and we exchanged numbers. I think I texted him first about a week later. The "Good to meet you, let's hang the next time I'm in LA," kind of thing. We exchanged texts here and there.

A few weeks later, I found myself up in LA hanging with some of my friends, so I reached out to him. We decided we would grab some food at Formosa, a restaurant in West Hollywood. It would be my first time hanging out with him. I kinda thought it was a date. I didn't know that he had just started seeing someone he had met on tour. All I knew is we had a really nice time. We ordered so much food, shared everything, and laughed a lot. It was definitely then that I began picturing myself with him, which is typical. I still have the fortune from the cookie I received that night. It read, "Kiss Me."

It's funny how our minds can certainly run away with themselves. It would be three years before we shared our first kiss.

I made it a point to go to LA a few more times to hang out with him. He never made a move, We ate and drank wine, we listened to music, we shared stories of life on the road. He got it. Again, there was no indication he was starting to get serious with anyone. One night, I stayed over because we'd had too much wine. I thought maybe something would happen. It didn't. And I was okay with that. I genuinely enjoyed spending time with him.

The next morning, after I left his apartment, I got a call from a publisher saying they wanted to publish my book. He was the first person I called. I was so excited—I wanted him to be proud of me.

And he was. He was gracious and congratulated me. I just couldn't tell if he was into me or not.

One of the last times I hung out with him before the pandemic, he mentioned a "friend" coming to visit. A couple weeks later, when I stopped by his apartment to work on music, there were plants all over the place. That's when I knew—it wasn't just a "friend." I wasn't dumb. He was seeing someone. And that was okay. He was my friend. I could accept that.

By now, it was spring of 2020. I was getting ready to leave for tour. I was at my bartending job for my final shift, watching the news on March 15th. My flight for pre-production was the next day. I was so ready to go. Then, Gavin Newsom came on the screen. California was shutting down. I got a call from Scooter—our tour was off.

I went to the back of the restaurant and tried not to cry. My boss asked if I wanted to leave early. I said no. I worked my shift. None of us really knew what COVID was yet. We just knew it was spreading and scary. We had no idea what was coming.

That night, as I shared earlier in the book, I got home to find a party being planned at the house I was staying in. I wasn't comfortable with that, so I packed a bag and moved to my best friend's farm. What I thought would be two weeks turned into six months.

I was making candles, creating music with her fiancé, helping with her Airbnb's, and working weird takeout shifts at the restaurant. Eventually, I left the restaurant altogether. During this time, I noticed some photos M was tagged in on IG. It was clear—he was in a relationship. With someone I kind of knew. She had messaged Cold's IG account. I didn't know her personally, but I judged her anyway. I was bummed. I liked him. But he chose her. I had to be okay with that.

At that point, I still hadn't fully cut ties with B. We weren't in a committed relationship, but we were still seeing each other throughout the pandemic.

The pandemic gave me time to finish my book with my editor. *Unfuckwithable: A Guide to Inspired Badassery* was released under Rose Gold Publishing in June 2020. One of the proudest moments of my life. Nearly 500 books sold in the first month, and that was with no real marketing. I had Tricia to thank for always pushing me to finish it.

Fast forward through the summer...Tensions started to rise at the farm. There was a lot of drinking going on, and Tricia and her fiancé were having their own issues. The time had come for me to leave. She had graciously let me stay for six months, but they needed to return to their normal life and work through things. Fallbrook felt too small. Plus, I was partying way too much and needed a break—or so I told myself.

I moved back to LA in August of 2020. Part of me was excited to be closer to M. I was still bothered by who he was dating—I knew things about her that didn't sit well with me. I always wanted to speak with him about it but felt it best to leave it alone. Eventually, I did bring it up, and he told me she had disclosed some things to him.

To stay friends with M, I had to accept him dating her. That led to dinner hangs with me, my LA besties at the time, him, and his girlfriend. I wanted to be around him, so I had to be around her. I was kind. I played along.

We hung out a few times. I did my best. That was that. I was living my life—selling books, making candles, and hanging with my crew in LA. He was living his life with his girlfriend.

It's now summer 2021. He still had one of my basses—I wasn't really using it, so he kept it for his music. I was prepping to leave LA for Indiana to do pre-production for our fall tour—our first post-pandemic. I needed out of LA. Tinder guy had burned me, and I was still reeling from all the lying. The experience had me at my limit.

M came by my apartment to return my bass. I was sniffling from a weekend bender, which had unfortunately become a weekend norm. Not proud of it, just honest. He joked about COVID. I told him it wasn't that—I'd just been doing blow after discovering more lies from that guy I had dated. M laughed it off. And he wasn't even interested in me. So, I didn't think it mattered. We hugged goodbye. I wouldn't see him again until February 2022.

I headed to Indiana and then out on tour—cue the disaster that was D. As I've shared, that was hell. Looking back still makes me nauseous. But the Universe has a keen sense of timing.

After that nightmare Costa Rica trip with D—the worst vacation of my life—I flew straight to LA to meet my friends from Chicago. We had tickets to Manchester Orchestra at the Hollywood Palladium, bought long before I met D. I wanted to see M on my trip. We were still friends. He had messaged me a week earlier, asking if I wanted to buy a house in Vegas with him. His relationship clearly wasn't going well. I remember thinking, *Is this it? Am I finally going to get a shot with this man I've dreamed of?*

I responded, "Hell, yes," joking, not joking. I already knew I wasn't staying with D. The signs were all there. I just needed time.

I asked M if he'd pick me up from the airport and join me, my best friend, and his girlfriend for dinner. I wanted them to meet M, and I wanted M to meet them. Ryan, my bestie in Chicago, owns the Legacy Hospitality Group—The Vig, The Vig West Loop, The Whale, and Welcome Back Café. These are all amazing restaurants. Go by if you're ever in Chicago. Ryan is one of my rocks. We're bonded through music and a million incredible moments that began in 2017. He's family.

M picked me up from the airport. We had an amazing dinner altogether. He dropped me off at my friend's apartment. I wouldn't see him again for months, but I was very happy to just be in his presence.

The attraction to M was deep. I still wonder—was it Tricia planting the *"he's your husband"* seed? Or did I just make him *the one* out of excitement? I didn't really *know* him, know him. But I wanted to.

We all long for connection. For someone to call home. I've rushed that feeling more than once, as you can clearly see. Damn patterns...

At that point, I was still technically in a relationship—one I wasn't thrilled with.

Not to mention, D was so jealous of M. As I had shared previously, I was ready to leave D when I was on tour in the spring of 2022. He was just way too much for me—and honestly, I had moved so fast and moved in with him so fast, I didn't even know what I was getting into. I just didn't like who he was as a human. I was so over all his narcissism. As I had mentioned, my plan was to move out as soon as I got back from tour.

This timeline overlaps with when D came to LA, despite me asking him not to. I had invited M to come to that show. I really wanted him to see the band. I wanted him to see *me*—performing, in my element. It's always important to me to have friends at shows, especially ones who know me but haven't seen me play. Being on stage is magic to me. You don't really *know* me until you've seen me live. Playing for Cold is one of the greatest gifts of my life, and I'm endlessly grateful to be part of this band.

That evening became a massive source of discontentment for D—but honestly, everything seemed to be a source of discontentment for him. Of course, *that* night would be. And of course, M would be. D would later scream at me, saying M looked at me all night like he wanted to fuck me. I didn't believe that for a second. M isn't like that. He's not some lust-after-a-girl kind of guy. He's way more chill, which is part of why I fell in love with him. He has this quiet strength about him.

I had never told anyone—except a few close friends—how I felt about M. At the time, regardless of what I was feeling, we were still *just* friends. It was still just a crush. If anything, it was the other way around. I lusted after *him*. The chemistry was obvious to anyone who saw us together. Even my singer noticed it and called me out.

M eventually broke up with his girlfriend. They weren't aligned—and yes, I may have been a part of the reason. I had planted a giant red flag in his mind about her. Sometimes I wish I would've just kept my mouth shut. But we hadn't crossed that bridge yet. That would come later.

M became a huge sounding board for me when I finally escaped that place on the East Coast. When I made it to the Midwest, I'd spend hours on the phone with him. He was now single. I was now single. *This is our chance,* I'd think.

I was doing everything I could to get back to LA. I missed my people. I missed my life. And I wanted to be near him. It felt like the world was opening with possibility. My new apartment wouldn't be ready until October 15, but that was fine. It gave me time to get my shit together—save up money, empty my storage unit and finally bring back all the things I'd left behind when I first moved to California back in 2016.

This was when the move from New Jersey to Indiana for the summer took place while I prepped to return to LA. During that time, one of my girlfriends was getting married in New York, so I made a trip out of it. I flew back to visit my east coast bestie, Kristina, and rented a car to drive upstate for the wedding.

During this trip, one of my dear friends, who is the tour manager for the band, Breaking Benjamin, hit me up and asked if I wanted to come out to their LA show. This show would be early September of 2022. I immediately said yes. I called M on my way to the wedding and asked if he wanted to join me and see if I could crash at his place, since I wasn't moving back until October, *plus*, I wanted to see my new place because they were putting in new hardwood floors. I also wanted to get the whole layout so I could get the furniture I needed. And duh, I wanted to see him. He said yes, and I booked my flight.

M picked me up from the airport, and I was so happy. Again, everything about him was perfect to me then. We got some food, we hung out. We drank margaritas. We slept in the same bed. Still, he had not made a move.

The following evening, we drove down to Irvine for the show. He had booked a hotel for us so we would have a place close by so we wouldn't have to drive back that night. He also was very intent on letting me know that he was totally cool with me staying later than him to hang with my friends. M isn't a 'hang out all night' kinda guy. I am. I love spending time with my friends. The BB guys also have the best karaoke after parties. I met M's publicist, and we hung out post show.

M and I had lots of fun at the show. I introduced him to my friends, and he also introduced me to some of his that were there. He decided he wanted to go back to the hotel after the show was over. I stayed, and the band arranged a driver to take me back to my hotel. M was asleep, so I took a shower and crawled into bed.

The next morning, we went and had breakfast and went to an outlet mall on the way back to LA. I loved every part of this. I picked out some super cute sunglasses for him that he bought, and in my heart, I just felt like this was the beginning of something special.

We had a nice weekend. I had a very early flight on Monday morning, so I scheduled my Lyft for 4:30am. I was getting ready and waiting for my Lyft and crawled back into bed with him while I waited. It was finally then, that he pulled me to him and was cuddling with me. I finally just turned around and we shared our first kiss. It made my heart stop.

My Lyft was not arriving, and I was in West Hollywood. I was supposed to board my flight in 30 minutes, and I was at least 40 minutes from the airport, so he got up and graciously took me. I ran to my gate and was the last person on the plane. But I had made it, and I was the happiest I had been in a long time. I had finally kissed this man I'd been wanting and waiting to kiss for three years.

Once I got back to Indiana, I was sorting and packing and had plans to meet up with Cold in Pennsylvania because we had a show in North Carolina that was on the books. It had been rescheduled twice already, so we were all a little leery, however, we had an obligation to fulfill. M and I were still talking every day, and I couldn't wait to move back.

The second Scooter and I landed in Pennsylvania, we got the call that the show was canceled. Because we were under contract, they still had to pay us. We just didn't have to go to the show. When I told M this while I was there, he suggested I fly back to California and spend some time there with him. I initially said no because I was literally going to be back in two weeks. However, since it was a band trip, the ticket was paid for, so after discussing it with my east coast bestie, she told me to absolutely go. So, I did. I hopped on a plane back to Los Angeles. This is now late September. I was moving back on October 15.

M picked me up from the airport, along with his business partner who had flown in to do some work. One of their clients was playing at the Hollywood Palladium the following evening and wanted to meet up with us. We met them at the Formosa. This was a full circle moment for us, since that was where we had our first dinner together. I felt like it was meant to be. We were giggling as we chatted about how it had been three years since we were there, and under very different circumstances. I felt like we were just beginning to get to know each other, and we'd finally been intimate. I went home a week later, renewed, excited, ready to show up for this man that I had wanted for so long.

CHAPTER 13

Almost Wasn't Enough

They say opposites attract. M and I were similar in many ways, but in the places that mattered most—emotional availability, communication, vulnerability—we were worlds apart. I was excited, magnetic, and wanted to soak in every drop of connection from the people around me. He was quieter, more reserved. I thought his calm was what I needed after the chaos with D. I didn't realize it would become its own kind of silence.

After our week together, I flew back to Indiana. Two weeks to pack, grab a U-Haul, and drive cross-country. One of my best friends flew into Indiana to make the trip with me, and we made it in record time. When we arrived in California a few days later, my friends helped me unload everything in a few hours. I was finally back home where I belonged.

M picked me up that same day. I was sweaty and exhausted but seeing him felt like coming up for air.

The beginning of us was a blur. I was all in—heart, soul, and time. He was still testing the waters. Within two weeks, after spending nearly every day together, he told me he had a date. My stomach dropped. Here I was pouring everything into this, and he was still unsure. Still deciding.

Instead of expressing how I really felt, I buried it. I pretended to be chill, "cool girl" chill—the kind who doesn't ask for clarity, who goes with the flow, who doesn't speak up even when her heart is breaking. I kept quiet. I drank to numb. And I would keep doing that for months.

I was always afraid my truth would push him away, especially this early on. I lived in my fears even then. Even though I taught otherwise. Even though I would give you the opposite advice. Looking back, I see it clearly. *He* wasn't sure. And I hated him a little for that. But that anger was wrapped in old wounds—feelings of not being enough, of always being the one who cares more. He had his baggage too. And I didn't want to rock the boat.

Then came the visit from his mom. He wanted to introduce us. I was so excited to meet this woman. I felt like I was going to make a new friend. That excitement quickly faded. I came in full of love and curiosity, but she met me with ice. I asked questions and tried to engage. She would answer coldly, as if I were wasting her time, and didn't even reciprocate the questions. She barely looked at me. I kept telling myself I could win her over. Maybe she didn't approve of my tattoos? I wondered, hearing the old stories from my father. But here I was again, practically begging for someone's acceptance. And M just said that was her personality.

Later that month, we flew to her place for Thanksgiving. It was just as cold. I felt invisible, but I kept smiling and kept my head up. *"Just give it time,"* I would think. The thought crossed my mind—wondering if she was wondering how long I would last for her son. He was turning 50 and still hadn't been married. Maybe she was just as cautious as he was. I would analyze this for years. I'll honestly never know. And it was also *never* just her personality. I saw how kind and interested she would be with other people right in front of me. It's as if she went out of her way to make me uncomfortable. I could sense it.

About two months in, we had our first "incident." His band was in town to play a show, and I was meeting most of them for the first time. We started the evening at his place with margaritas with one of his guitarists, who had just arrived from the airport. I was buzzed and carefree. Later, at their Beverly Hills rental, I was laughing, goofing around, making friends. I accidentally tripped over M's foot and spilled my drink. I think I even put my hand in his face in a playful way.

He didn't laugh. He took me home. And the ride home was silent disappointment besides him telling me I embarrassed him.

I walked into my apartment and collapsed in tears. I had ruined everything. I didn't think he'd want me at the show the next night. I felt like a disgrace. He made me feel like everyone thought I was out of control.

But the next day, I apologized. I bought him a gift. And when I saw the girls again at the show, they looked confused when I apologized for my drunken behavior. "What are you talking about? You were totally fine," they would say.

M saw one version of me. Everyone else saw another. I believed the girls. Was this my first-time experiencing shame with him?

That night, I did a bump of coke in the bathroom at the Rainbow. I asked the girls not to mention it. I knew M wouldn't approve. But at that point, I wasn't living for my own values, whether they were good or not—I would try to shape myself into the version I thought he could love.

And that's when I started to lose myself.

I had been intentional about not partying like I used to. M didn't approve of any drugs like that. And because it didn't ever alter my behavior besides sobering me up if I was drunk, I didn't want to be judged by him about it. I've never been an addict, but I partied. I have always been a fan of moderation because my health is important to me. I know that sounds like an oxymoron. I totally get that, but it worked for me. I never considered myself to have a problem with drugs. I could take it or leave it. M wouldn't find out about this incident until a year and a half later, which we will get to.

The rest of the weekend went off without a hitch. They had a photoshoot the following day in Beverly Hills, and we barbecued. Again, everyone had a great time. It's so interesting to me to see now how afraid I was of "messing up" and losing this human. I would constantly blame myself and shame myself. He wasn't even committing to me, which was also one of the reasons I would drink. I tried to numb the feelings I had. If I knew then what I know now, I may have walked away much faster than I did. There was always a pressure that if I didn't live inside this perfect mold, I'd be out. And that terrified me.

The holidays came and went that year. He went to visit his family out of state, and I stayed back to take care of my friends' home and dog. Due to insane storms, we didn't get to spend New Year's Eve together.

The second incident came a few weeks later. I'm sharing these major things because they are important to the story. And you shouldn't have to try to be perfect to keep someone or attempt to get them to fall in love with you. Love doesn't work that way. If that's the case, you are not in the right relationship. Period.

At this point in time, I still didn't know where we stood. He never posted about me on social media. We weren't "boyfriend and girlfriend." When he was away for those two weeks over the holiday, we spoke every day, but anytime I would say, "I miss you," he would never say it back. There wasn't much intimacy, and I was beginning to wonder if I was wasting my time. I felt like he was keeping me at arm's length. That drove me nuts. There were nights I would be staying with him and cry myself to sleep after he'd fall asleep. I didn't feel there was a reciprocity of feelings.

But even so, I would clean his dishes, help tidy his home, and put things together for him. He never asked me to do these things. It was just a natural inclination to show I was not lazy. To show him I was worthy of his love. I knew I didn't like how I felt. But I kept thinking that if I could prove myself, he would love me back. I see now I was sort of taking on a mother role—and I don't want to mother a 50-year-old. Gross. But this was my participation in the game of *"Choose me, I'm great!"* I felt like if I could show him how motivated I was, he'd do just that.

Back to the incident: We went out because one of his friends was in town to play a show. I started doing shots and drinking heavily. I've come to realize now that any time I do shots when I'm feeling unfulfilled inside, it never ends well. Actually, shots in general never end well.

We were at the Rainbow on Sunset Strip, post show with the band. I had taken off with his PR agent to do a shot at the bar. She asked how things were going with M, and I said something personal—and a bit crass—about how we'd been fucking for months but weren't in a relationship, and I didn't know where we stood.

M overheard me but didn't say anything until later.

I was at a peak of frustration. Feeling undervalued and not chosen made my self-worth plummet. Drinking made me forget about it for a while. It allowed me to push the truth out of my head: He wasn't going to commit to me. He couldn't even say he missed me.

We were five months into dating by now. And once again, I had embarrassed him. He dropped me off at my apartment that night. I honestly thought it was over. Again. Broken. Again. Beating myself up. I cried myself to sleep that night, wondering why I was always messing things up.

The next day, we had a heart-to-heart. He said he wasn't ready for a relationship and wanted to be free to travel and do what he wanted without having to answer to anyone. He also let me know he overheard me speaking to his agent, and he didn't appreciate that.

And I get it—I shouldn't have said what I said. But I didn't have the strength or clarity to walk away. Why had I not learned my lesson from B? Still, I was out to prove myself. I'm a recovering people-pleaser. I've built a history of giving way too much of myself without reciprocation.

My best friend Tricia—who had introduced us—had moved to Texas. She'd been asking me to come visit for a while, and I never did because I wanted to spend every minute with M. But after his comment about not wanting to be in a relationship so he could do what he wanted, I'd had enough.

I booked a ticket to Texas.

I left a few days later. While I was there, Tricia and I had an extremely healing moment. We had been estranged for a couple of years after a fight we had. We finally had the chance to go all-in and discuss what had happened in 2021 and forgive each other. It was a big deal.

While I was in Texas, M and I talked on the phone. One of the nights, Tricia and I had a couple of margaritas with dinner. When I spoke to M that night, and told him I missed him, and he once again didn't say it back, I had pretty much had it. Like, why could this guy not say I miss you to a girl he spends literally every day with? I confronted him about it. He asked me if I was drunk. I told him no, because I wasn't. I told him I had had two margaritas a couple hours ago. He then flipped it and asked if I was sober. Well, I said yes, because I was. But then he said I was drinking so I was not sober. It was truly a ridiculous conversation. He was not answering my question and rather putting it on me, saying I was drunk. I felt defeated here. Again, I couldn't get it right. I'm a grown-ass woman and can't have a couple of drinks and express my hurt when someone can't even say "I miss you?"

The next morning, I was so upset. I was crying. I was pissed. I also had a photo shoot that day, so I couldn't be a mess for that. I texted him, saying, "we need to let this breathe." He took it as "I was breaking up with him." Well, we weren't even together. Didn't he recall the conversation about not wanting the responsibility of a relationship? Then he sent me a text that wished me best of luck in everything I did. That was that. I was in shock and was so upset. Once again, blaming myself. But I let it go. When someone tells you to have a nice life and good luck with it all, that is finality. So, I let it go. He no longer wished to engage with me.

I returned to LA, heartbroken. Those couple weeks before I left for tour were brutal. I was crying every day. I drank every night and worked on music. I drowned myself into everything I could to not think about him, all while preparing for a huge tour. When I wasn't playing music, I would be a wreck, blaming myself for not being good enough for him. Blaming myself for drinking. Blaming myself for everything. The mentality I had about myself did not change for a long time. It was all my fault, and I was a fuck up. It's now March of 2023. We had only been dating six months. Again, he couldn't even say he missed me. We barely had sex. He never kissed me. I knew I needed to mourn this loss and move on with my life.

I then made a tragic mistake of looking at his ex-girlfriend's Instagram account. I wondered why he had posted photos of her on his IG and not me. What was I missing? What was so wrong with me that he would never post me? Let me just say something right here, right now about this. If a man does not choose you, do not, I repeat, DO NOT go down the rabbit hole I went down. It made me so depressed, *insanely* depressed. I was literally comparing myself to someone 20 years younger than me, who's IG was a compilation of a girl with perfect breasts, a perfect body, all these things, and she wasn't afraid to show it off. Comparing yourself and your worth to someone else's Instagram account is not healthy. I'm an adult, who is in a popular rock band, the author of a book about being Unfuckwithable, yet here I was, COMPLETELY fuckwithable. It was not a good look. And it certainly didn't feel good.

So, what did I do? Everything I could to numb the pain. I pretty much had friends over every night of that two weeks keeping me company, making sure I was okay. I have the best friends on the planet. I knew I needed to get sober because our tour was starting in two weeks. I'm typically in the best shape for tour. I was not at the start of this one. I was a little chunky from drinking so much and not getting adequate sleep, even though I could barely eat. I felt like I ruined the best thing of my life.

I had put M on a pedestal for years and continued to do so since we had begun dating. The truth is, he didn't belong there. He was not perfect. I was not perfect. At this point in my life, he had let me go, and I wasn't going to fight for someone who was so easily dismissing me and wouldn't commit to being with me.

When I was leaving Los Angeles, I was in my little seat on the plane next to the window, sobbing. I could not stop crying. So, I busted out my first book and started re-reading it. I figured I needed to maybe look back and take my own advice on everything. I always knew *Unfuckwithable* was a powerful book. It helped, but the pain was still there.

When I got to Pennsylvania, I focused solely on being healthy. I had decided to clear my head and scale back the alcohol because I wanted to drop the weight I had gained from my bad decisions. I didn't eliminate it completely, however, I committed to getting my head in the game for this tour. It was going to be a grueling one as we were doing 54 shows in 10 weeks, in addition to the tour being an anniversary tour, and we had two new members. I was doing my best to be in the moment, but it was obvious to everyone that my heart was broken. And it was. And I blamed myself. I hadn't spoken to M in weeks, and everything reminded me of him.

Broken. Shame. Guilt. My fault. If only I would have made different decisions, would things have turned out differently?

CHAPTER 14

Loving Him
Was Losing Me

We headed out for tour. About a week in, while I was playing in New Hampshire, I got a text from him. I was completely caught off guard. He said he didn't like how we'd left things and asked if I wanted to talk. I felt like this was my moment. I was ready to do whatever it took to get him back. We talked the next day and continued to Facetime throughout the rest of the tour.

He was home working on new music for his band, and I was on the road with mine. I did my best to give him as much of my time as I could. That's when I started noticing little quirks. One came out while I was in Jacksonville. I mentioned that his agent had reached out and would be coming to our LA show. He wasn't thrilled. He made it clear he didn't like me talking to his friend—and when I sent him screenshots of our messages to prove she'd reached out first, he still seemed skeptical. I found it odd that he had made such a big deal over it.

But I was all in. Being with him was the only thing I was focused on. Even when things felt off, I didn't say anything—afraid he'd lose interest again. If it had been anyone else, I'd have blocked their number and moved on without a second thought.

I don't know what that pull was. I had mostly cut out drinking on this tour, and I made a point to tell him since it had caused problems before. Still, one night I had drinks with friends who came to a show—and it became an issue. Again.

I felt judged. Like I had to explain every decision I made. Through therapy, I've since learned that when I feel judged, I revert to my teenage self—and that triggers rebellion. He said he wasn't upset that I drank, but he was upset because I had said I wasn't going to, and I had. It was all so silly to me, yet a big deal to him. He was seeing his own red flags. I can own that.

Still, I hadn't seen him in months, and I missed everything about him. And now, finally, he was saying he missed me too. He had his own shit to work out—though I don't think he saw it then.

We started planning a time to see each other. The original idea was for him to come to our show in Tampa, where his drummer lives, but his schedule didn't allow it. Eventually, we landed on a plan: after our final Texas show, I'd fly to Phoenix on our day off, and he'd meet me there. One of his best friends offered us his house to stay in.

The plan was for me to meet the band at soundcheck in Scottsdale, play the show, and then spend one more day with M before flying to San Diego together. He'd ride with us to Anaheim for one of our shows and then back to LA because we had a show there, and that's how he'd get back home.

In the week leading up to our reunion, he had second thoughts about coming. I begged him not to back out. Eventually, he stuck to the plan.

Seeing him again felt warm and comfortable. I couldn't explain why being next to him always felt so right. I wanted another chance—to show up differently, to love better, to finally build something real with him.

In the month leading up to Phoenix, as we'd been working through things, we finally decided to give a relationship a real shot. I knew we both still had kinks to work out. I was ready for a fresh start. I wanted to give him a chance to show up differently, too.

We had a good week together. He came to my shows, spent time with my band family, and he even flew to Las Vegas the next weekend to see us play a big festival. We met up with my friends from Chicago and he finally met my best friend, Brandy. I was on top of the world.

I still had three weeks left on tour, but for the first time ever, I was excited to go home—not because I was tired of being on the road, but because I missed him. The tour had been amazing, but this time, my heart was ready to be with him.

When I got home, we were officially a couple. He was committed, and I was ready to give it my all. I always was. We were happy—at least it looked that way on the surface. We spent nearly every day together. He was my best friend. We did everything side by side.

But there was one thing that gnawed at me: we had been together for nine months, and he *still* hadn't posted a single photo of us. Not one. He never acknowledged me publicly. It stirred something in me. Was he hiding me? Was he not proud of me? It became a running topic with my best friends. We were rarely intimate. We barely kissed. And I kept asking myself if I could live with this kind of relationship if nothing changed.

Side note: I know I keep mentioning this posting thing. There was something about it that hurt me. Every single person and couple that I know shares their loved ones publicly, in *some* capacity. He had for his ex. He had photos with other people. Why not me? It *really* bothered me.

A couple months after tour, his band was ready to start laying down tracks for the album they had been creating. He'd been writing while I was away, and now it was time to bring the band together in Florida to start recording. The trip was set to start on my birthday. I was so excited—this was supposed to be a beautiful time.

We took a red eye the night of the 20th. My birthday is the 21st. I know he was tired, but he planned nothing special for my birthday. I'm a big birthday person—I always have been. And all I really wanted was something simple: a public happy birthday. A post. A photo. Anything. But I got nothing. He passed out after spending the day in the studio and didn't even come to my birthday dinner. I tried to wake him. But he stayed in bed, wouldn't move, and I went out alone with the others.

The next day, I was feeling a little melancholy. What made it even worse was that I had posted a photo of myself wearing his band's hat in my annual birthday selfie the day before. He didn't even *like* it. But when I opened Instagram, I *did* see him like a photo of someone he used to date—a woman he was still friends with. And she had *just* posted her photo 30 minutes prior. So, it's not like he didn't see my photo. He *ignored* it. That crushed me. I confronted him. He brushed it off and made me feel small for even caring. He said I was too focused on social media, said it didn't matter, and asked me some bullshit about how I would feel pre-social media. But it mattered to me. And instead of listening, he turned it around, like I was the one being unreasonable.

Two of the other guys had brought their girlfriends, and we tried to enjoy the time. The girls and I did spa days, went out, hit the beach, tried to stay light—but underneath it all, I felt invisible to him.

One day, while we were there, one of his friends came by, and we had all gone out to dinner and had a night on the town. He had a boat and offered to take us all out. That's something the girls and I were interested in doing. The guys were busy in the studio, and M's drummer suggested we hit him up. I didn't have his number, so the drummer gave it to me. I took it—but then thought better of it and deleted it. I knew M's stance on me being "friends" with his friends. It was ridiculous, but I didn't want another fight.

But we had one anyway.

He accused me of flirting with the guy the night before and accused me of wanting to be with him. Full-blown meltdown. He said it was *my* idea to call him, when it wasn't. My girlfriend had to step in and tell him, "I was there—it wasn't her idea." Still, I found myself begging him to look at me. To believe me. To talk to me like a human being. I hate how pathetic that sounds now. My anxiety was at an all-time high. I almost booked a flight home.

His insecurity was spiraling. And no matter how much love I gave, it never seemed to be enough. I had zero desire for anyone else. None. And yet, he treated me like I was untrustworthy. Eventually, he apologized, but the damage had been done. I was gutted. I don't know how we made it through those ten days, but somehow, we did.

We got back to LA, and once again, I buried my feelings. I just wanted peace. I had a tour coming up in September, and M's band would be heading out in October. It was a big moment for him—his first time back on the road in over a decade. And despite everything, I was happy for him. It was an exciting time for both of us. I always encouraged him and his music and to continue pursuing it. I was so supportive of that because I know how it feels to do this. And I knew he missed it.

I left for tour. This one was only a couple of weeks. We spoke every day, and I did everything I could to stay in communication with him, and I didn't drink at all. Once I got home from my tour, I went out with him on his tour. I wanted to be there for support, and I also wanted to be there to sell his merch. I wanted to be on his crew and thought I would do the best job at it. I'm a hard worker, plus, I have fans that would come if they knew I was in town. I was constantly posting videos, sharing on my social media that I was going to be out there with him, and did all I could to help promote his tour. I didn't bring in TONS of people, but I did bring in some. I also sold so much merch. Everyone was impressed with the numbers, despite the shows not having the greatest attendance.

We survived the tour. We got along really well. I wanted to be helpful. He had a bout with COVID on the tour also, and I did everything I could for him. I felt like I was still trying to prove my worth. Like this voice in my was head saying, *"Oh, if he can see how dope and cool you are on the road, he'll respect you more."* The thing is, I don't feel like he ever really respected me. Maybe fleeting moments, but the bad was beginning to outweigh the good. What was I even doing?

I lost my day job while I was out there with him. I had been working remotely, part-time as an office manager for a NYT bestselling author for nearly three years. Her business model was changing a bit, and she was shifting to AI strategies to save money on staff. These things happen. And if I were being honest with myself, it was getting hard to work a day job and be on tour at the same time for years. However, it helped pay my rent and by now, I had been back in LA for a year, and no one was paying my bills for me.

Financial stress was starting to weigh in. I was in a bit of credit card debt from my cross-country moves and having to furnish an entire apartment, but I had faith everything would work out. I made some money on his tour and had money coming from my tour that would get me by. He referred me to a telemarketing job that I could do from home. He used to work with the company, and I was grateful for the lead. I was hired. My job was to help sell subscriptions for shows in Los Angeles. I started my training in November.

We traveled to see his mother for Thanksgiving. This would be my second time being at his mother's home for the holiday and his birthday. I still felt unwelcome. I knew that she didn't care at all for me. It had not been easy with her. My mom even noticed it when she was in town earlier that summer. Our mothers were both in LA at the same time, so we took them to Venice Beach, and we went out to dinner one evening. My mom told me to just keep being me.

I did my best to rise above how I was treated, but it doesn't take away from the sting you experience when the second person you want to like you, doesn't even try to get to know you. I would ask her questions about her and get one-word answers and then silence. She never attempted to build a relationship with me. The entire situation was so weird. To cope, knowing this, I focused on my writing and my candle business when we would go there.

We got back to LA, it was now the beginning of December.

I am going into some of the lowest lows of our relationship: I spent every night at his place, hoping he'd touch me. Hoping he'd kiss me. Hoping to hear that he loved me. Hoping he'd let me in. My friends would ask me that if he didn't know he loved me after a year, what was I doing? I was getting really good at hiding my sadness with him and sharing my true feelings with my close friends. He would say he was depressed. And I wanted to be there for him and not leave just because it was hard. I would keep telling myself this would pass.

We were coming up on Christmas, and one of my girlfriends was having a holiday party. We got dressed up and went. After we left, I felt like I was so tired of walking on eggshells and holding my emotions in, so I finally said it first. I told him I loved him. His response was that I was just saying that to control him. While I was deeply hurt, I still did not leave him. *"He loves me. He'll say it one day,"* I would say to myself.

He wanted to go back to his mother's house for Christmas. She had a bunch of office stuff he was going to be helping her put together at some point in the next few weeks, plus she was going to be alone. He wanted to surprise her. He didn't like to drive on the highway and asked if I'd drive. I didn't want to go, but in my head, I was once again thinking, *"I'll prove that I love him by driving him to the one place I never felt comfortable. If that doesn't show loyalty, what does?"* Yeah, I know…That makes complete sense. I even stopped to get her flowers. I wanted this woman to accept me so desperately. I still longed for his approval. I still longed for her approval. I wanted everything to be beautiful. My heart was being shattered, I didn't deserve the way I was treated, and I felt like I was being taken for granted. After that trip, I made a promise to myself that I was never going to go somewhere I didn't feel loved or wanted again. That was it for me. I never went back. I had finally created a boundary. One I was proud of.

The next few months were a whirlwind. I began nannying for my best friends' daughter and trained to be a chair technician for the NBC show *The Voice*. I was also working and making calls for the company he referred me to (I *hated* it, but I was good at it), and I was starting to prepare for my upcoming Spring tour. I thought it was best that I focus on me and started spending time at *my* apartment. I was slowly beginning to pull away in my heart, but I was still there physically, though not as often, in every possible way.

Months pass, he still had not posted me on his social media. Add to the fact that I would tag him in photos, and he wouldn't even approve the tag to show on his own page. But he would with other people. It was making me sick. He still was not initiating any sort of intimacy with me. And I was still trying to show him I was worthy. I was slowly dying. My dreams of us were slowly dying.

One of his friends reached out to me after I wished her a happy birthday and asked if M and I wanted to meet up with her and her guy for dinner because he was going to be in town. I said yes and told M about it. I was berated, once again, about how I shouldn't be talking to his friends. My patience was wearing thin, and I was becoming super depressed. My friends started seeing it. I was not in a good place. We went out one night, and I had enough alcohol in me to stop stifling my voice. I confronted him again on why he never touched me. On how I was feeling no sense of worth from him. I felt like we were just best friends, and he was only keeping me around because I was a comfort to him, and I helped him do shit. And he didn't have to be lonely. I felt so low. And angry. I ended up leaving after that conversation and going home because he once again, did not hear me. He said he goes through "phases."

All the while he had such a big issue with me speaking to his friends, I was encouraging him to be friends with mine. M had been considering venturing into a project that one of my friends has expertise in. They had been discussing this. However, this was and is one of my closest friends. When I left M's apartment that night, I was so low. I drank half a bottle of tequila and cried and cried. The next morning, I talked to my friend who was helping him. I told him I had left M and filled him in on how angry and hurt I had been feeling.

I felt like I was ready to be done. I was tired of feeling unloved and unwanted. I was giving my everything to him. The next day, M had a scheduled meeting with my friend, and my friend told him he was not comfortable helping him anymore. M seemed shocked. I also had some time to cool off and think. So, I sent M an email with all the issues I had, telling him nothing was unfixable. I was still hoping for a different outcome.

M kept asking what I said to my friend, and I didn't dive into the details. I kept saying, "Nothing, it's just bad timing," because I was still trying to reconcile everything that was happening and was still afraid to lose the relationship. I wasn't completely honest up front. I wasn't honest about a lot of things, especially when it came to my feelings. I had too much fear surrounding me and surrounding him breaking up with me.

When I would bring up how I was feeling, nothing ever changed. His answers would always be the same, like, he's depressed. And I would still give and give and get nothing I truly needed in return. We did not speak for a couple days. However, because I was leaving the following week for tour, we mutually decided we wanted to spend it with each other. I was still so in love with him. I wanted with my entire being for everything to be different. I wonder if that's where I just broke. I wonder if this is where I gave up.

I left for tour. This time, I decided I was not going to drink. I had already scaled way back in that regard. I went most of the tour with no alcohol. We all, the band, wanted to put our best foot forward, on top of the fact that that it was a co-headlining tour. We had always been the headlining act, but wanted to see how this would work out. For the first couple of weeks, I would talk to M, and we would Facetime, but every time I did, he wouldn't even have the phone facing him. I would be staring at a ceiling, and there would be some excuse as to why.

About two weeks in, his ex-girlfriend that I had the insane amount of insecurity about, came to a show we were playing in Portland. I saw her from the stage. It looked like she was fighting with her boyfriend, and he left. It was weird, but after the show, she was by herself, and I happened to walk by her. I decided in that moment that I was going to face my insecurity of her and just say hello. I went up and said hello, and she said she and her boyfriend had gotten in a fight, and he left her there and didn't know where he was. I don't know what came over me, but I wanted to take her under my wing. I felt sorry for her. So, I said, "Hey, do you want to meet Scooter?" Her face lit up and she said yes.

She came down with me, and Scooter was hanging with everyone outside the bus, so I introduced them, as they had not met in person. We all chatted for a few. Her boyfriend finally responded to her and let her know where he was, and she left.

M lost his shit over this when he found out from her. I also did not know he still spoke with her. Another punch in the gut. I honestly felt like I did nothing wrong here. He accused me of some bull-shit. And hung up. We were done. He broke up with me. And at this point, I threw my hands up in the air. I couldn't continue like this. I was over it. All the bare minimum shit, and he was breaking up with me for being nice to his ex? Okay. I get it. I am not the one.

I did not call him when we got to California. I didn't invite him to any shows. I don't even remember when he reached back out to me. But I was done fighting. Then he began reaching out a lot. He had started coaching with someone and was learning about some deep fears in him that he had been avoiding. He was trying to share this with me on tour, however, I was over it. I didn't want to talk to him. I didn't want to hear it. I wanted to focus on being on the road. I wanted to be happy and not have the constant stress of how he was going to be, or how he was going to react, or hear how he was judging me. I wanted peace.

When we did finally speak, and he shared with me all the things he was seeing, it was enough to give me some hope. He finally said, "I love you." But I was still feeling insecure about all of it. I reluctantly decided to work on things with him. He was being more open. He said things would be different when I came home. There was a defi-nite shift with him. But honestly, I was angry. Why now? Because I was done? Because he didn't want to lose me?

I did not give him the attention he wanted or thought he deserved while I was on the road. He was angry with me most of the time. He said I didn't care. I was honestly just feeling beat down. I wanted to enjoy myself and be in the moment. Then his head got away with him. He took my silence for hiding. He assumed I was hooking up with someone from the band that was co-headlining with us. Noth-ing was further from the truth. I cried every day. I missed him every day. The on and off was killing me.

At some point, he had found out I did blow in the Rainbow Room that year and a half prior after his show with his friends. Someone told him. And I admitted it. It had happened so long ago. And yes, I told him I did ask them not to tell him and the reasoning behind that. He made a very big deal about this. Once again, my behavior in my past was coming back. I was still begging for him to see my worth.

When I got back from tour, we decided to give it another go. I had been invited to a friend's party the first weekend I was back. It was out of town, so the plan was to spend the night. I invited him to come, even though that was not the original plan since we weren't together when I was asked. But he came.

My friends work hard and play hard. I did a couple of bumps at the party because it was around, and I was on edge with M. No one knew. I was in a different room. I wasn't out of character. I was fine. He wanted to go to bed at like 10pm, wanted me to be with him, and there was a party going on. He was upset because I wanted to hang out and not go to sleep right then. I was beginning to think everything was always about him and how he felt. There were so many things that had to go his way, and if not, I was being selfish. We got in a huge fight that night.

The following day, he asked me if I had done drugs. I lied at first, and then finally said I had. He wanted to break up with me. Out of some crazy desperate move, I told him I was an addict and needed help. I did not fucking need help. I never have. I'm not an addict. I was so afraid to lose him. Here we were again.

In my pleas and appeals, we decided we would seek couples' therapy. I then totally took back what I said about being an addict. I felt like I was backed into a corner, judged so harshly from this human. I felt like he continually looked for evidence of me fucking up. It didn't feel like love. It honestly felt like he didn't even *like* me.

It was a rough summer. That incident took place the first weekend in June. The following weekend was my best friends' daughter's birthday, whom I nannied for. He was invited. He decided he did not feel well and opted out of going. I had not seen my friends since be-fore tour. I consider them my family here in LA. They also had their family in from out of town. I had some drinks, we were all in deep conversation, so I decided to just stay the night. I didn't feel like it was a big deal because his boss was in from out of town. He blocked me that night.

Another fight ensued about how selfish I was once he finally un-blocked me. How HE wanted to spend time with me and wanted me with him. I could not catch a break. We'd make up but there would always be *something*. But we were still pushing through.

My birthday ended up falling on the same day my band was play-ing a three-day festival in Ohio, so M and I would not be spending that day together. We spoke that morning and he wished me happy birthday. Not a big deal. We had a show to play. This festival had 75 thousand people in attendance, and I was ready for it. It was such a magical day. Scooter surprised me by having the audience sing Hap-py Birthday to me. It brought me to tears. I literally felt like one of the luckiest girls on the planet. It was the most memorable birthdays of my life. And yet, I was still hoping for a special post from the man that I loved, who said he loved me.

I was busy the entire day, running around, hanging out with friends, and seeing some of my favorite bands that were also playing the same day. I am lucky enough to have thousands of people online, who celebrate with me and give me birthday love. When I would take a break from the socializing, I would be able to see *some* of these posts as they came up. I responded to a few here and there, but it takes me days to actually see *all* of them and respond to everyone.

Rather than posting a photo of me, or doing anything on his own page, he decided to write happy birthday on my Facebook wall. He didn't tag me. It got buried. I hadn't seen it. I hadn't even seen half of what was there. By the next morning, he was so upset that I hadn't responded to *his* post, yet had responded to others, that he said this was why social media was so stupid and he's never posting anything for me again.

I was in shock. Was I dealing with a child? Scooter literally saw the change in my face though I was trying to hide it. I was on my tour bus, trying to keep it calm, letting M know I hadn't even seen it yet, but he went on and on. Here we go again. Scooter asked me what was wrong. I couldn't hold back the tears. Though I finally got through to him that I literally hadn't seen the post, the damage was already done. More hurt. More resentment. Nothing special, yet again.

It would turn into months of stupid things like this. We were in and out of therapy. Back and forth, disagreeing about who wasn't doing what and where it all went wrong. There was a toxicity that was turning into a vicious cycle of hurt and pain for the both of us. When our therapist would give him feedback or challenge him, and he didn't like it, there would be times he'd walk away from the on-line session. We'd go weeks without speaking, only to fall right back into a few perfect days, and then I'd do something to upset him.

I had to come to accept that this was something I could not sustain. I could not make him the number one priority *all* the time, like I had in the past, at the expense of myself and my relationships outside of ours. He did not like my friends. He would make comments and judge how other people treated me while taking zero accountability for how *he* was treating me. The people in my life are important to me. And for so long, I let many of my friends and my own goals, go by the wayside. I don't want to be that kind of friend. I also don't want to be the person who pushes things off to tomorrow, and I had been doing that way too often. I did my best to find a balance, but nothing was enough.

Through all of this, I realized that my fears didn't just revolve around how he viewed me. I also had all these fears around what other people thought. My friends and family could see the slow decline of my mental health. I was not happy. I was in a constant state of worry and fear. I was walking on eggshells in all areas of my life. With him and with my friends who were tired of seeing me hurt. So, each time we got back together, I wouldn't tell anyone, because I felt like it was just a matter of days or a week before we would be on the outs again.

He was never physically abusive to me. He has never laid a hand on me. I was never afraid in that type of way. We both carried past trauma into the relationship that we obviously had not healed from. We both had a fear of abandonment. We are both highly aware individuals, and we're both smart and levelheaded most of the time. We looked very good on paper. I didn't understand why this wasn't clicking like it should be. I was so in love with him. I guess I was more in love with what it *could* be. This clearly wasn't it. Sometimes, when you work so hard on something and it's not going the way you wanted, there is a sense of failure. No one wants to feel like they've failed at something. Neither of us wanted that and we both kept trying to fix each other. It's impossible to do that. I should have known this by now.

My best friend, Tricia, asked me why I didn't just leave. I remember answering immediately: I had an underlying fear that he'd suddenly heal and then give all the love I had longed for, to someone else. FOMO – Fear of missing out. And somewhere in me, I didn't think that was fair, considering all the time, effort, and pure love I had put in. It was a devastating thought at the time. I was holding on for dear life, making up a fake scenario in my head to justify my efforts.

The rest of the year would be a roller coaster of ups and downs until he broke my heart the day after Christmas, texting some of the worst things to me, because I had stayed up late where I was housesitting, drinking tequila and learning songs on my bass. His anger toward me was unwarranted. I had never experienced that type of cruelty from him. The things he said were meant to break me, diminish my worth, and make me feel bad about myself. In addition, the words were entirely untrue.

I knew then that this was not love, at least not from him.

CHAPTER 15

From Self-Sabotage to Self-Love

"Enlightenment comes to those who free themselves from self-oppression."

— BRENDON BURCHARD

"Nobody wants to do it—not real change, not soul change, not the painful molecular change that's required to truly become who you need to be. Nobody ever does real transformation for fun. Nobody ever does it on a dare. You do it only when your back is so far against the wall that you have no choice anymore."

— ELIZABETH GILBERT

I'd love to tell you that was it—that I was finally done. But I wasn't. I went back after 55 days of no contact.

In those 55 days, I was heartbroken, still felt so much love for this man, but I was also slowly rebuilding. I was gluing the pieces of myself back together. I could feel how much I'd shrunk—how I'd boxed myself in to keep fitting into something that was never meant for me. And I was finally starting to see that he would never give to me, the love I had given to him.

Over two years together, and not once had he publicly supported me—not one post, not one mention, not one share of my band. Meanwhile, I'd shared him everywhere, hyped him up, and stood by him through everything. When that realization sank in, I deleted every trace of him from my social media. The shame ran deep.

I decided to reevaluate my relationship with alcohol. This time, I wasn't doing it for him. I was doing it for me. I'd used alcohol to numb the pain, to smooth over the red flags. But no more. I needed a fresh start, and finishing this book became my priority. I'd been working on it for 6 months prior to this, and I never quite knew how the story with M would end. Deep down, part of me still held out hope. I still wondered if we'd make it. I wondered that if enough time passed, we'd end up together.

Then, on February 19, we ran into each other at a show in West Hollywood. I was nearly two months sober and feeling proud of the work I was doing on myself. I had a headlining tour coming up, and we were playing two full albums in their entirety. Shows were already selling out. I was rehearsing every day, working out every day, writing every day—I was healing.

When I saw him at this show, the chemistry was still there. Undeniable. But chemistry is not compatibility. Don't let it fool you.

We gave it another try. I still blamed myself for our past blamed my drinking and my mistakes. But now that I was sober, I could see things more clearly. He told me he had slept with someone during our breakup. He said he wanted to *"feel wanted and desired,"* and that I *"wasn't there."*

I sobbed.

It wasn't even about the act so much—it was the hypocrisy. For two years, I'd begged to feel wanted and desired, and he'd called me insecure. He told me I shouldn't need validation. But now that was *his* excuse? It was bullshit. And it broke me all over again. Even in our separation, and my thinking we'd maybe end up together, I stayed true to my feelings for him. I couldn't even think about going out with anyone, though I was asked.

There was never anything *special* with me—not in the way he made me feel. This last round ended just like all the others. Only this time, I wasn't going to be gaslit. I wasn't going to be the one apologizing. And I wasn't going to be the one to blame.

He wouldn't give me what I needed. That would require much more work. It became so clear—he did everything he could to push me away. Even the smallest things.

There was one moment while I was on tour that changed everything for me. And it's so dumb but spoke volumes: He was watering my plant for me while I was away. I asked him if he'd talk to her while he did—just a silly little thing. I always talk to my plant. I tell her how beautiful she is, how proud I am of her growth. I asked him to do the same, just while he was watering her. His response when I asked him again, after he had said no, with a *please*: "I'm not going to talk to a fucking plant."

That was it. That was the moment. A small ask, one that would make me happy—and he couldn't be bothered. It told me everything I needed to know.

We officially ended things two weeks after I came home. No big fight. He left for his mothers to help her do some things around the house. This gave me some space to really think about what was going on. I decided I would use the confidence I had been building and have a talk with him when he came home. He called me on a Sunday while he was there. He asked if I thought we were growing apart. I said yes and asked if he felt the same. "Yes."

I told him I actually wanted to talk with him when he got back. He asked, "Why bother?" That was a bit crushing, but I honestly didn't expect anything else from him. He said he didn't have the energy anymore. Too overwhelmed with his band, with money.

Okay. You don't have to tell me twice. Begging Lindsay is gone. Proving her worth Lindsay is gone.

If he *really* loved me and wanted to be with me, real change would be required. But I wasn't on his priority list. My needs were definitely never on there. It was obvious. And mere presence was not enough for me.

I will no longer accept breadcrumbs.

And yes—it hurt. I had to sit with the reality of not being chosen again. But this time, I also saw it for what it was: the death that makes space for a rebirth.

Sabrina Zohar said it perfectly:

"Staying because of history is just dragging your past into your future. Sometimes love isn't enough. If they can't meet you halfway, it's time to walk away. Letting go isn't failure—it's freedom from a cycle that isn't serving you. You deserve someone who chooses you without hesitation, not someone who keeps you waiting. Closure isn't something they give you—it's the decision to stop chasing it."

I once again found myself asking why I stayed as long as I did. Why any of us stay when we're not being honored, respected, or loved the way we ask for.

But I know now: I thought love had to be earned. I thought if I just loved him a little harder, held on a little tighter, it would become what I dreamed of.

But as Matthew Hussey said, *"Chemistry isn't compatibility. Attention isn't intention."*

Someone's presence doesn't mean they're choosing you—it might just mean you're convenient, and I certainly was. The truth is, we mistake pain for proof it was real. We tell ourselves the good moments outweigh the slow death. That we can survive the heartbreak—as long as we're not alone.

But self-worth doesn't whisper. It roars. It doesn't beg to be chosen. It *chooses itself.*

I don't shame the version of me who stayed. She loved with her whole heart. She hoped with everything she had. But I honor the version of me who finally stopped begging and walked away. The one who realized being *almost loved* isn't love at all.

Looking for Love in All the Wrong Places

All relationships have one thing in common: **Ourselves**.

It's not fun to take inventory of our own behaviors, thought patterns, or the ways we show up (or don't). But if we're failing in our relationships, chances are there are other areas where we're falling short too. One of the most important things we can remind ourselves daily is that we have to put in the work—whether it's on ourselves, our relationships with others, or the life we say we want.

I've always dived headfirst into relationships. And boundaries? I don't think I ever really had any. To me, a boundary was just "don't cheat on me." And even then, I settled more than I'd like to admit. I know now that I've been in love with being in love. I craved acceptance—craved it like air—from someone else. It was something I had longed for my entire life.

It stung when I finally realized how often I'd been abandoning *myself.*

In her book *It Begins With You*, which I believe every human should read, Jillian Turecki describes the dynamic I've found myself in so many times:

"Whenever our need for someone's love is stronger than our self-love, we will abandon ourselves in the pursuit of their attention and validation. We'll try to win their love even if it's the wrong love... The person whose attention we are so hungry for is usually the person who does not deserve our love."

"You are not here to chase people. You're not here to wait by the phone, perform for love, or prove your worth to anyone. The longer you chase someone who's unavailable, the more unavailable you become to the life you were meant to live."

"When you're caught in that loop—chasing love, hoping, proving—your world starts to shrink. Your big, beautiful dreams get smaller. You begin to orbit around their availability. And every time you pursue the unavailable, you give away the time, energy, and presence that could've gone toward building the life you were meant to live."

My entire MO in relationships—and honestly, in life—was to just "go with it." But coasting is not creating. We roll with the punches rather than boldly shaping who we want to become and what we want to see in our world. We don't set boundaries because we're afraid of rejection, but the truth is, we're rejecting ourselves every time we do that. Wouldn't life (and love) be easier to navigate if we actually knew who we were, what we stood for, and placed a high value on our own integrity?

Even in manifesting. Manifesting is beautiful. Vision Boards are great. The Law of Attraction is powerful. But none of it works without the work. It's easy to dream up your ideal life. It's easy to write the list, set the intentions, and visualize the dream. But when the gap between where you are and where you want to be, feels impossibly wide, it's just as easy to give up. Especially if you don't feel you're worthy of it. Maybe I never felt I was. But I finally dropped that story I was telling myself.

Mel Robbins talked about this on *The School of Greatness* podcast. She said that instead of focusing solely on the end goal, we need to visualize **the bridge**—the in-between. The long nights. The boring days. The consistency. The healing. The discomfort. The silence. The action. That's where the transformation happens.

The bridge, for me, has been this growth journey.

Letting go of fear. Sitting with myself. Learning how to be alone again—not lonely, *alone*. And what I've discovered along that bridge has been both horrifyingly sad and beautifully liberating.

Self-Sabotage

I've been the queen of self-sabotage. Now that I know this about myself, I've learned to watch my thoughts, actions, reactions, and patterns more closely. It's been a recurring theme in my life—compromising my health and well-being with alcohol and drugs, procrastinating by binge-watching shows instead of taking small steps toward my goals, judging others without examining myself, comparing my path to others on social media and feeling like I'd fallen behind.

I've hated my body. I've shamed it. I've let people take advantage of me. And even after all my accomplishments and all the inner work, I've still struggled to *really* love and accept myself. I've been my own biggest problem. But the beauty in that realization? I can also be my solution.

I might be spiritual, meditate, and coach others, but for a long time, I still sabotaged my own progress. I'd move forward, only to backslide, over and over again. And the hardest part? Realizing it was me. I was the one keeping myself stuck.

Also—I do not feel like I am a victim. I am taking full accountability of my participation in every situation I have found myself in. M saw his own red flags in me. I was no angel, and I was drinking a lot in the beginning. It was normal for me and my friend group at the time. Had I not, would he still have been as hesitant? I don't know.

Choosing sobriety this year was the best decision I've ever made. Truthfully, you probably wouldn't be reading this book if I hadn't made that choice. At least not right now.

I kept repeating to myself, "If you want something to change, you have to be willing to do something different." That phrase helped ground me. It inspired me to make a different decision. And it applies to *everything*. If we're in a toxic relationship, if we're stuck in a job we hate, if we have a dream we're not chasing—we're part of the problem. And until we own that, we stay in cycles that rob us of our potential. Self-sabotage is a sneaky little bitch.

I came across this post by Branden Collinsworth that hit me right in the chest:

- *Self-sabotage looks like choosing toxic when you know what's healthy.*
- *It looks like avoiding opportunity out of fear of failure.*
- *Pushing people away because you're afraid of being vulnerable.*
- *Overthinking until you miss the moment.*
- *Creating chaos when you finally find peace.*
- *Settling for less when you know you deserve more.*
- *Clinging to the past instead of being present.*
- *Not speaking your truth because you're scared of hurting others.*

Self-sabotage is the voice in your head that convinces you you're not ready, not enough, not worthy. It's the invisible chain keeping you from the life, love, and joy you deserve. But here's the truth: self-sabotage doesn't stand a chance against self-love. Real self-love means you love yourself enough to struggle. You embrace the challenge because you know it's shaping the version of you who is free.

We're creatures of habit—sure. But we're also creators of our lives. And only we can rewrite the habits that hold us back. Every single day, we have the power to choose a new thought, a new belief, a new way of being. As Brendon Burchard says, "Motivation is conscientious." It's effort. And that effort is *so* worth it.

Alcohol was a problem for me. I used to deny it, pretend it wasn't a big deal. But it was. It made me angry, insecure, and most damaging of all—it disconnected me from Source. I either held my feelings in or drank just enough to let them all erupt. It stole my motivation, made me procrastinate, and dulled my energy. It chipped away at my self-worth because I kept betraying myself. I was sick. I was tired. I was anxious. And I was done.

On January 2, 2025, after a day of sobbing and nursing a hangover on New Year's Day, I asked myself: *What if I could love myself enough for one year?* What if I made *myself* the priority—for real? What if I stopped trying to prove my worth to everyone else and focused on my own healing, my own dreams, and my own alignment?

So, I quit. I forgave myself. I gave thanks for the wake-up call. That relationship crash didn't break me—it cracked me open. It showed me this wasn't about being "not enough." It was about my patterns. My silence. Ignoring my intuition. My habit of shrinking to keep the peace and searching for validation outside of myself.

Not anymore.

I also needed to address the underlying fear that I wouldn't have a good time without alcohol. That maybe my creativity would dry up without it. The truth is, alcohol is the most dangerous and destructive normalized drug out there—and it's everywhere we turn.

This isn't some anti-alcohol rant. I have no problem being in social settings where people are drinking. I don't mind when my friends or family drink around me. And who knows—maybe one day I'll have a margarita again, or a glass of wine. But not today. Today, I'm choosing differently. Because this is what's best for me *right now.*

What I *will* say is that more and more studies are coming to light—studies that show there's no amount of alcohol that's truly safe. The more I learn, the more grateful I am for this shift. I can't begin to tell you how much better I feel every single day—waking up refreshed after *real* sleep. My workouts have improved. My body has changed. I'm stronger. I'm more motivated than I've ever been. I've got this renewed sense of purpose and excitement that meets me every morning.

I don't beat myself up anymore. I don't carry shame. Because I know that right now, in this moment, I'm giving it everything I've got—and that's planting the seeds of an unwavering confidence inside of me.

This has required a serious pivot in my thinking. A deep commitment to living in integrity with myself. But here's the thing— you *can* forgive yourself. You *can* live free from the things that once held you back. Every single day is a chance to begin again, no matter where you are.

And let me remind you: **You are worth it**.

Taking Accountability Without Guilt and People Pleasing

Another essential part of breaking our own toxic cycles is realizing we are in control of our lives—and that taking accountability for our own bullshit is *excruciating*. Trust me, it's not something we're all screaming from the rooftops.

It's so much easier to point the finger at others and claim they're the problem. One of my biggest issues was giving too much weight to what others—especially my ex—thought of me. I preach about being unfuckwithable, about not giving a damn what people think, and yet I was still someone who deeply cared about what people thought. I hadn't truly dug into the guilt piece, especially when it came to being a lifelong people pleaser. For me, it was either extreme people pleasing or full-blown rebellion. Both were rooted in guilt—this deep, underlying fear of disappointing someone.

Here's what I've learned: We all have our own shit. The people we choose to be in relationships with carry their own insecurities, wounds, and baggage. I've been impatient. I've been defensive. I've gotten offended (cue the scoff: "How could you even think that about me?"). I've been angry and resentful. A lot of that came from childhood wounds. Many of my relationships mirrored the dynamic of a parent/child. So, like I did as a kid, I would hide behind perfectionism, because I didn't want anyone to shame me or think less of me. Or I'd over-function, diving into a caretaker role to prove my worth.

The truth?

I was a liar. And a manipulator.

I didn't fully grasp this until I read *The High 5 Habit* by Mel Robbins. It punched me in the gut—in the best way. She wrote:

> *"Pleasing other people is great if that's what you truly want to do, and it makes you happy. It becomes a problem when you start betraying your own needs for the fear of other people being upset with you... As a people pleaser, I will do anything to manipulate your emotional reaction. I use the word manipulate on purpose, because I knew it would bother you. People pleasers think they're being "nice."*
>
> *Nope, we're liars. If you're a people pleaser, you will behave in a way to manipulate what somebody thinks about you. That's why you spend most of your energy curating yourself so that you fit in, or will be liked, or so that no one's mad at you. You are manipulating what people think about you. Instead of just showing up as yourself and making decisions that work for you, you twist yourself in knots so that other people won't be upset with you."*

Yeah. That stung.

But I needed to hear it. I'd rather face the uncomfortable truth than live in a comfortable lie. And this was a truth that freed me.

In my last relationship, I felt like my autonomy was slowly being chipped away. And instead of expressing that, I hid. I hid drinking. I hid my occasional drug use. I hid the aching fear of not being enough. I even hid certain insecurities to play the role of the "cool girlfriend." I muted my feelings so I wouldn't be "too much."

At one point early in our relationship, he made a comment about how I always brought up my book or my band when meeting new people. And I noticed myself being a little quieter after that—dimming my light in social settings. But those things? They're what I'm most proud of. Why wouldn't I talk about them? My work is my life, and it's something I want to share. That comment planted seeds of self-doubt I didn't realize were growing.

Love doesn't try to quiet you. Love doesn't ask you to be smaller.

Those moments—and there were many—weren't about me being "too much." They were about his insecurities. But I couldn't see that at the time. I was too caught up in trying to stay. In not rocking the boat.

You cannot have a healthy relationship if you're hiding, people-pleasing, lying, or manipulating. And you sure as hell can't have one if you're too afraid to have uncomfortable conversations. That was my downfall. I was terrified to lose him. Terrified that my full self would be too overwhelming, too complicated, too flawed.

I had to ask myself the hard questions. What did I truly want? Who did I want to be? And was I living in alignment with that? I read a quote Erin Schaden posted on Medium that stuck with me:

"Anything you lose by speaking your truth isn't a loss. It's alignment."

That hit deep.

So now, I choose alignment over approval. I'm learning to speak up, even if it's scary. To live in integrity. To be unshakable in my truth. That's where self-love is built—through conviction. Through resilience. Through the refusal to hide anymore.

If what you want doesn't align with someone else, you owe it to yourself to be honest about that. Move on. Or commit to doing the work. But don't pretend, don't perform, and don't betray yourself just to be liked or chosen. That is so basic.

We're not here to be basic. Basic is boring.

Values

I had to get honest about my values. What truly matters to me?

What do you value most?

How does your purpose align with the way you're living right now?

Who do you want to be?

What do you want to do?

Here's what I've come to know about what's important to me on this healing journey:

1. My purpose. My faith. My goals.

Living in alignment with what I'm meant to do on this earth is everything to me. I know I'm here to serve. Whether it's performing, writing books, coaching, sharing blog posts, or sending out raw, real-life newsletters, sharing my journey—my intention is to inspire others to go after what lights them up and live a life they love. My spirituality is the foundation. It's braided into my purpose.

2. My health.

Since choosing sobriety, I've placed an incredibly high value on my physical, mental, and emotional health. Every day, I move my body, I meditate, I journal. I carve out over an hour to set my mind and energy right. I go to bed early because I wake up early—my body's rhythm is consistent, and I honor it. Sleep, for me, is sacred. When I'm taking care of myself, I can fully show up—for me and for the people I love.

3. My relationships.

When we're clear on our purpose and taking care of ourselves, we can show up for others from a place of abundance—not obligation. When we neglect ourselves, love turns into resentment. I know this truth intimately.

4. My growth.

You don't evolve once and call it good. Growth is a daily, conscious commitment. I read books, listen to podcasts, and surround myself with voices that challenge and stretch me. Sometimes I need to hear the same lesson over and over—from different people, in different ways. I'll never again date someone who doesn't value personal growth. It's a non-negotiable for me.

We must learn about ourselves, work on ourselves, love and accept ourselves.

Because the longest relationship we'll ever have is the one we have with ourselves.

And if we haven't sorted out our own stuff, it's hard to show up in a loving relationship—and way too easy to be manipulated by those who also haven't sorted theirs.

That Self-Love Part

We hear all the time that we must love ourselves. It all makes sense, right? Of course, we should. But knowing and doing are two very different things. How do we do that? How do we get to a point where we aren't beating ourselves up for all our perceived imperfections?

I spent years beating myself up—never feeling like I was enough and constantly shaming my body. I've suffered from body dysmorphia since I was a child, and it only got worse as I got older. I became obsessed with how my body looked, with how I was perceived, shrinking myself for some impossible standard.

This began back in the '80s. I've always been an active girl. I ran around, rode my bike with friends, spent hours at the public pool, climbed trees like a tomboy, and played *light as a feather, stiff as a board* at pretty much every slumber party ever. You know, all the classic Gen X stuff—before cell phones and the internet were even a thing. I had a pretty great childhood in that regard.

I never thought about my body or weight. I'm athletically built. But in grade school, many of my friends were petite—much smaller than I was. I started noticing the difference early. I remember sitting next to my best friend, Lori, in chapel; she'd cross her legs and I'd do the same, but mine would raise higher than hers. I started to notice... and compare.

I must've been around ten years old when I was first body-shamed—for no apparent reason—by my sister's best friend, who was always at our house. She was such a bitch. (The same one who shamed me while I was in the bathtub as a young girl.) She made a comment about me being fat because I couldn't see my toes. That moment stayed with me. After that, I started sucking in my stomach in every photo. I started obsessing.

I talk about this more in *Unfuckwithable*—like the time in middle school when a boy made fun of my nose and my lips. I thought something was wrong with me. I started biting my bottom lip in pictures to make it look smaller. I wanted a nose job. I'm so grateful I never went through with it.

But body-shaming wasn't just in our peer groups. It was *everywhere*—especially in the popular tabloids we consumed like religion. Here's an example of what we were seeing growing up:

Fashion victim of the week

Oops! We forgot to put Mariah Carey in our "Fat Thighs" story! On those porky pins, the pop princess is no dainty "Butterfly." Her va-va-va-voom Versace couldn't be much shorter — it's barely bigger than a T-shirt! Why doesn't the suddenly single songbird just go naked?

(Tabloid image taken from Instagram: @alexlight_ldn)

What the actual fuck?

Eating disorders became a thing. We were starving ourselves. Binging and purging. Watching every calorie. Over-exercising. All to live up to some unrealistic, white-knuckled version of perfection that was never even real in the first place—and definitely not sustainable.

As I shared earlier, when I lived in Terre Haute and Gainesville and drinking a ton of beer and started gaining weight, I got up to the heaviest I'd ever been. I was only 20, but I had already started hating the way I looked in the mirror. That shame led me down a dark path—a bulimia stint that lasted around six months. I'd binge a pint of ice cream and then throw it up. Atkins was all the rage then, so I lived on tuna, meat, cheese, and mayo. Then I started throwing up more often. I was abusing my body. Abusing my mind.

Eventually, I hit a point where I knew something had to change. So, I started walking and jogging. I'd dance in my room. After I moved to Tampa, I joined an all-female gym and hired a personal trainer. I just wanted to feel better. I wanted to *look* better. I lost about 15 pounds in 3 or 4 months just from moving every day. But even then, I still thought I was "fat."

Even now, at 47, I have moments when I look in the mirror and think, *"You can do better."* While I'm nowhere near as obsessed as I used to be, I still go there, especially if I see an unflattering photo when I'm on stage—just not as often.

Last year, I did a massive unfollowing spree on Instagram. If a post made me feel bad about my body or my journey, it had to go. I no longer wanted to subscribe to shame and the comparison.

These days, I make choices that feel *good*. I walk every day. I lift weights most days. I move my body not because I hate it—but because I *love* it. Because it feels good. I want to be strong. I want to feel good on the inside and the outside.

Cutting out alcohol has been huge. I'm not pumping my body with all that extra sugar, and I'm no longer missing workouts because I'm hungover. It's not about being perfect. It's about being kind to myself. Showing up for myself. Honoring this body and this life I've been given.

Self-love is being kind to ourselves, even if we aren't exactly where we want to be in *all* areas of our lives. It's that gentle pivot. It's saying, *"You've got this."*

Imposter Syndrome

Imposter syndrome is deeply tied to self-worth—or the lack of it. I've wrestled with this more times than I can count, especially being in the music industry and writing books that I hope actually help people. I've had thoughts ranging from *"Who the fuck are you?"* to *"There are so many more talented people out there—better writers, better musicians..."* You name it, the thought has probably crossed my mind.

But here's the thing: that pivot is *everything*. The difference between the people who just dream and the ones who *actually do the thing* is action. *Inspired* action. Everyone starts somewhere. Every icon, every trailblazer, every badass—started where you are. Doubt and all.

And seriously—how are *they* (the people you're comparing yourself to) helping you? Are they making you more enlightened? Helping you hit your goals? Making you feel stronger or more at peace? Probably not. You are the only one who has power over your choices, your thoughts, and your growth. You don't need anyone's permission to take up space or own your story,

Now, let me share something that Gary Vaynerchuk said when someone asked how to handle being undervalued, being overlooked or when people doubt your leadership ability in your company. If you're offended by the *F word, you may want to skip this section. I'm leaving this exactly as it is (transcribed), because it resonated so profoundly, and maybe it'll do the same for you:

"The first two is you quit. You know, this is the same old shit. If you don't like your job, if your boss thinks you suck, if you don't like it...if you don't feel valued or validated, live on fucking Indeed until you get a fucking new job. You know, people just love rolling in their mud. I feel like the world is just a bunch of hogs and pigs, you know those animals love the mud. You know when you go to the farm, you see the hogs, they just fucking roll in that mud and you look at their face, and they're just fucking happy. Unfortunately, that's what a lot of people in life are like. People just want to roll in their mud. They literally live in complaining about their husband every day, live life complaining about their job, their wife, their girlfriend. They love to point fingers about how their older brother or younger sister got lucky, or they have it so good. Stop rolling in fucking mud. New York City says life is tough or life is easy. Simplify your shit. Take control. Do you know how many people are much happier right now than they've been historically? Because this last political cycle they were just like 'I'm just not even going to pay attention.' They took control of what they consumed and thus they were less anxious and less upset.

And then the third one is stop valuing other people's opinions when you go somewhere. And people that make you feel lesser than? Fuck them. Why the fuck are you looking up to celebrities? Why the fuck are you looking up to businesspeople that made more money than you? What are we looking up to? We completely lost our way. We used to look up to our grandpa. We used to look up to fucking religious figures, right? You know who used to be famous in 1950 in America? Pilots and astronauts and politicians. Now it's people who are selling sex on apps. Yeah, I went there. I mean, what are you looking up to? Don't look up to me because I'm good at making money.

Look up to me because I treat people nice. Don't look up to me because how many followers I have. Look up to me because I'm sitting here trying to add value. Don't fucking give a fuck about any room that doesn't want you there. Fuck that room. Don't put a room on a pedestal. Fuck that room. If a room doesn't want me, they fucking lost, I promise you that.

Your self-esteem is broken. You're not confident enough that you can get another job. You're not confident enough that you're better than the room... I've been in every room. And guess what, I don't give a fuck about any room I've ever been in. Not the biggest boardrooms in the world, not the Oval Office under both administrations, Republicans and Democrats. I don't give a fuck about the room. I respect the room. I'm empathetic to the room. I understand the room. But fuck the room. I'm not letting anybody make me feel lesser than. I go to a fucking event. Do you know how many events I go into where I don't get into the VIP and the people in the VIP's have less money than me, less clout than me? Listen, it doesn't even go through my fucking mind. Good for them. I'm happy for them. You think a velvet rope matters? People, enough!"

Mic. Drop. 🎤

It's raw. It's real. And it's exactly the energy we need when we're second-guessing our own value.

Here's the truth: the road to hell is paved with *well-meaning advice.* Every time we doubt our gut, every time we play it safe, every time we let "reality" (or someone else's version of it) box us in—we're handing over our power. If I had listened to every person who told me to play small, to get a "real job," to stay in my lane—I wouldn't be here. And I'm damn proud of how far I've come.

I believe reality is bendable. I live by faith. I believe in the quantum. I'm of the Dr. Wayne Dyer school: *"When you believe it, you will see it."*

I've had plenty of people roll their eyes at that. And to every doubter, I say: *"Okay."* I'm not here to convince anyone. I'm here to live out my purpose and boldly follow what I know in my gut. I am the one who controls my thoughts, my choices, my energy. And I won't let anyone dim that ever again.

Yes, imposter syndrome creeps in. Yes, fear still shows up. That's human. But now, I know how to pivot. I know how to fight back with new thoughts that align with the woman I'm becoming.

Reframe the bullshit:

Old thought:
   "I'm not good enough."

New thought:
   "I'm worthy of greatness simply because I exist."

Old thought:
   "What will people think?"

New thought:
   "I will follow my excitement and my joy."

Old thought:
   "What if it doesn't work?"

New thought:
   "But what if it does?"

Old thought:
   "I can't do this."

New thought:
   "Let's break it down and take one bold step at a time."

Old thought:

"I'm not like [insert name here]."

New thought:

"I'm on a one-of-a-kind journey. And I can't wait to see how it unfolds."

Old thought:

"I'm not lovable."

New thought:

"I love myself first, and everything meant for me will follow."

These are the pivots.

The conscious decisions to think differently—even in the moments when we don't fully believe it. Because if we can convince ourselves that someone else will change, we can damn sure convince ourselves of something we repeat over and over again.

Our Mind Will Play Tricks

Something I experienced firsthand is how hard it is to break free from a dream you've built in your head—especially when that dream doesn't match reality. One thing I had been missing in the world of spirituality and the Law of Attraction was this: releasing the outcome and allowing. I'd come to realize I was doing a lot more forcing than allowing. More pushing than flowing.

I held onto an ideation for so long that it began to have power over me. The dream of *us* ultimately became my enemy. And I think that's why we hold on so tightly to something that doesn't feel good—because we're determined to make the outcome *mean* something. We put in so much time, and then our ego comes in and demands we make it worth something.

My friend Sarada told me early on, "It's like breaking a habit." And it was. I was in the *habit* of him. The back and forth. The proving. The trying. The abandoning of myself. I had a determination I couldn't see through clearly. I ignored and stuffed down the things that bothered me from the very beginning, and those things became seeds of resentment and insecurity. Even more so when I had the courage to bring them up, only to have them be brushed aside.

This started early. I had no idea how much of myself I was hiding in this relationship. Not consciously. I wasn't trying to be someone else—I was trying to protect myself. I was afraid of rejection. I now see this began early on when I was trying to fit in with my elementary group of friends. Trying to get the bullies to accept me!

Gabby Bernstein's *Self-Help* cracked me open. She talks about Internal Family Systems and the different parts that show up in us. She writes:

> *"There are two types of Protector parts: Managers and Fire-fighters. Managers often run the show, and these are commonly the parts that are with us on a day-to-day basis.*
>
> *Examples of Managers could be parts that strive for control in an effort to feel safe, or critical parts that judge others to avoid feeling judged.*
>
> *In situations where life becomes challenging and our Managers' protective techniques no longer work, a Firefighter steps in. These are the impulsive, numbing behaviors—self-harm, substance abuse, disordered eating—that 'extinguish the flames.'"*

I cried when I read that. I realized I had been protecting the part of me that feared rejection—by putting on a mask of perfection. Deep inside, I was panicked. Insecure. Screaming. Because the truth was, I *wasn't* secure. And I damn well wasn't perfect.

And that's when my Firefighters would show up. The numbing. The drinking. The occasional drugs. That voice would whisper, *"No one can tell you what to do. You're an artist."*

Even when I was trying to be "good," I was still judging myself. Even when I was better *comparatively*, I was still beating myself up. And yes—he shamed me for those things, and he was a catalyst for change—but ultimately, I changed for *me*. The shift happened after we split, and I was no longer doing it for anyone else.

There was a spiritual element to it, too. I believe in the Universe. I believe in divine timing and divine detours. I *know* life is happening for me, not to me. Even the heartbreak. And yet—I was resisting. I kept fighting what I *knew*. I saw signs. I felt the disconnection. I still fought it.

When we almost broke up after that one tour—because I told him I'd done some drugs—I panicked. I told him I was an addict just so he wouldn't leave. But that wasn't the real addiction. *He* was. I was addicted to *him*. And like any addiction, you seek your fix, even when it makes you feel worse. Even when it doesn't make sense. You believe that just *one more hit* will make everything better.

Matthew Hussey's book *Love Life* says:

> *"Letting go of an old love story starts with resetting what it is we actually value in life. And to do that, we need to decide what a love story worth having actually looks like."*

But I *loved* him.

He also reminds us how easy it is to hide behind love:

> *"Fear of being alone, addiction to the cycle, the belief that we need them to survive, the glorification we use to justify short-changing ourselves."*

So, I asked myself—what was I hiding from? What was I glorifying? Why was I still hooked on this person, even in the face of constant anxiety and misalignment?

Hussey also points out, *"It only takes a moment to create an entire epic in our mind of what this love story should be."*

Wow. I fucking did that. I created all the things in my *mind*.

And now, I let them go.

There are two sides to every story, and he has his own. I spent years trying to *make* it work. I'm done trying to figure him out. I'm done trying to analyze his behavior and pick it all apart. That chapter of my life has closed.

CHAPTER 16

Reclaiming the Magic

One afternoon, I was hanging out with one of my best friends, Nicole, whom I've mentioned often in this book. I love her so much, and we have so much in common. One thing we *don't* share, though, is her obsession with reality television. She was watching *Caught in the Act: Unfaithful*. If you haven't seen it, it's a reality show on MTV–BET where people who suspect their partners of cheating, get help from host Tami Roman, relationship expert Kevin Carr, and private investigator Brianne Joseph, to gather proof. Sometimes, they even confront their partners *mid-act*. It makes for dramatic TV, I guess, if you're into that sort of thing.

What struck me most was the desperation—how far some of the betrayed would go to keep their partners.

Now, I don't know how *real* the show is, but I *do* know I was yelling at the screen:

"GET OUT!"
"LEAVE!"
"FUCK THIS!"
"WHAT? YOU WANT TO WORK IT OUT?!"

It was maddening—and humbling. Because I've been that girl. I've been in that place where all logic evaporates, and you're left bargaining for someone to just love you right.

When you're the one *in it*, it's easy to lose yourself in the emotional investment, in the time you've poured in. But here's what I've come to know for sure:

We should never have to beg someone to love us.
Or to see us.
Or to stay.
We are *already* worthy.

If someone makes you feel like you're too much or not enough, it's not love. If they belittle you, try to dim your light, or make everything about them—it's not love. If someone continually puts their needs above yours or is constantly looking for what's "wrong" with you, it's not love. If they stop kissing you, stop touching you, stop lifting you up—it's not love.

I've ignored red flags in the past in the name of love, in the name of potential, in the name of feeling like I needed someone to *complete* me and not abandon me. But what I see clearly now is this: the only person who was ever abandoning me was *me*.

Love is a choice, and I was choosing everything but myself.

Actress, Megan Fox recently said, *"No amount of wishing will turn inconsistency into commitment, indifference into care, or toxicity into love."* And she's right.

We can't fix people.
They're on their own journey.
We're on ours.

The truth is: real love won't find you if you're not ready for it. You have to *complete yourself first*. Because once you truly love yourself, there is no need to chase it. And you won't accept disrespect, deception, or breadcrumbs.

And speaking of breadcrumbs...

According to Dr. Elizabeth Fredrick, breadcrumbing is a manipulation tactic used by emotionally immature individuals who give *just enough* attention or affection to keep you hooked—but never enough to truly meet your emotional needs.

She breaks it down like this:

- They say how much you mean to them, but their actions don't match their words.
- They show up *just enough* to claim they were "there for you," but shift focus back to themselves.
- They never clarify if the relationship is casual or serious, keeping you in limbo.
- They "change" just long enough after a conflict to keep you from leaving, only to slip back into old patterns.
- They act confused when you express needs you've voiced a dozen times.
- They deflect with their own stress or struggles instead of taking responsibility.
- They accuse you of being needy or ungrateful when you want more effort.
- They make *you* feel like you're the problem—too reactive, too critical.

And here's the kicker: some don't even realize what they're doing. But *intent doesn't* negate impact.

Dr. Fredrick says, "When someone genuinely cares about you, they are open to feedback. They put intentional effort toward healing. And they *try* to meet your needs—even if they don't fully understand them yet."

So, if, after multiple hard conversations, things aren't changing, it's time to let go.

You're not crazy.
You're not needy.
You're not unworthy.

You've just been conditioned to overlook your own needs. But that ends now.

Yes, people *can* change. I've changed. And I know what it takes—radical accountability, a willingness to face yourself, and a commitment to growth. Not everyone wants to go there. Not everyone is meant to grow with you.

And that's okay.

Because this is *your* life. And if you want something extraordinary, you must make room for it. You must release the people and patterns that are holding you back.

That's not giving up.

That's self-respect.

I believe that everyone who enters our life is there for a reason—to wake us up, to stretch us, to remind us of who we really are. Growth rarely happens when life is easy. It happens when we're cracked open, and still choose to love, to heal, and to rise.

Not every relationship is meant to last. But every relationship can teach us something that leads us home—to ourselves.

Keeping a Soft Heart

It's tough, man. It's tough to keep a soft heart when you've been hurt. The *audacity* of giving too much of yourself to someone who didn't return it can easily harden your heart, allowing bitterness to crawl in and take up a home. It's easy to replay the hurt over and over again in your head. It's easy to talk about it with your friends and let the story spiral into madness. It's easy to talk shit and badmouth. Been there. I've also seen plenty of messy, emotional social media posts that scream, *"I'm in pain!"* (Maybe keep that private.)

When anger and resentment show up? Pivot. Feel it—feel it for as long as you need. But then remember who the fuck you are. Marinating on the scenes that broke your heart when you didn't know any better is not worth your peace. That's being stuck in the past.

That's not to say the pain won't randomly creep in. There will be triggers. And it's definitely not about ignoring the pain. Quite the opposite. Sit with it. Cry. Scream. Go to therapy. Get it out. Give yourself time to heal. Reflect on what you missed—or on what you *didn't* miss but ignored. Be grateful for the contrast because it brings you closer to what you *do* want. You get the chance to reframe your future and reclaim yourself.

I spend a lot of time reading books. Earlier this year, when I was knee-deep in the core of my hurt, I read *The Motivation Manifesto* by Brendon Burchard. Books are powerful—they shift my focus from hurting to growing. I had spent the better part of two years completely distracted from my goals and dreams, consumed with trying to make a relationship work. I did that. No one asked me to. All my *own* doing. So here I was, being called back to myself, being asked to take responsibility for my own life.

In this incredible book, he asks:

When is the last time you looked inward rather than succumbing to the constant distractions that conspire to keep us unfocused?

1. *Am I proud of the person I am becoming?*
2. *Am I happy with what I am doing and contributing to the world?*

3. *Have I felt grateful for this day and its opportunities?*
4. *Have I directed myself purposefully so that I can live my highest truth and serve my highest good?*

I want to answer *yes* to those questions every single day. I don't want to be distracted by the bullshit.

Grow, Bitch! Grow.

Learning to Be Alone

There's been a lingering stigma around being single. I've talked to countless women who are desperate in their search for love or their "happily ever after." If we're not careful, loneliness can turn into desperation. And desperation is the first ingredient in a recipe for disaster. You can hop on any streaming service and find endless stories of betrayal from people who just wanted love—people who craved it so deeply they overlooked the endless number of red flags. It's heartbreaking, but it's also a wake-up call: not everyone has the same intentions as you do.

That's why learning to be happy in being alone is crucial. It's about giving *ourselves* the kind of love we once searched for *outside* of ourselves. That's where true self-worth begins. When you let go of what's no longer serving you, you allow space for what *does*.

From a young age, I was subconsciously programmed to believe that marriage was the ticket to acceptance, to security, to "home." I had to shed the idea that I needed someone else to complete me. I had to let go of the belief that I needed a partner just to create, or even to buy a home.

Reality check: I can buy my own home. I can create my own life. I can earn my own money. Every resource I need to build the life of my dreams is already within reach—and the same is true for you.

I complete me.

My circle—the people I love—support and uplift me, but they don't define me. When I think back to the nonsense I've put up with—things that made me feel small, invisible, or insignificant—I must remind myself to pivot those thoughts. To remember: everything happens for me, not to me. I wouldn't be here today, sharing this story, if these things hadn't happened. I wouldn't be this strong. And trust me when I say they do come up. Every single day. I know they'll dissipate with time. I'm still healing.

It's my responsibility to return to love for myself and to see all the abundance already in my life. If I can stay in that space of gratitude and faith—believing that beautiful things are coming as long as I stay open to them—then my future is limitless.

I finally recognize the patterns I've lived in. And now, I choose to move forward consciously. I know what I want my life to look like. I know what I want my *love life* to feel like. My job is to do the work, align with my truth, release the outcome, and let the Universe do Its thing. My responsibility is to consciously create a life I'm in love with *right now*.

A perfect example? My journey in the music industry. For most of my life, my dream was to be the frontperson in a rock band. But now? I can't even imagine that. I still get to be in music. I still get to perform. But I'm doing it a *different way*—playing bass in Cold, which brings me so much joy and fulfillment. It might not have looked like the dream I held in my head, but it's even *better* than that dream. The Universe knew my heart and brought it to life in a way I never could have imagined.

We don't always know what's best for us. But we are constantly guided and protected. Our job is to align with that guidance, so we recognize the blessings when they come. If something works out? Amazing. If it doesn't? Also, amazing. If we're waking up every day living a life we love, rooted in gratitude and trust—*regardless* of what we have or don't have yet—the Universe will bring more of that to us. That's law.

And speaking of laws, here are a few you should know:

Laws of the Universe

- **Law of Vibration** – Everything is energy. What you *feel*, you attract.
- **Law of Clarity** – Be clear about what you want, or the Universe won't know what to deliver.
- **Law of Action** – Manifestation needs movement. You've got to meet the Universe halfway.
- **Law of Belief** – You attract what you *believe* you deserve.
- **Law of Focus** – What you focus on expands. Choose your thoughts wisely.
- **Law of Gratitude** – Gratitude multiplies blessings.
- **Law of Alignment** – Your thoughts, feelings, and actions must align with your desires.
- **Law of Detachment** – Let go of how and when. Just believe it's coming.
- **Law of Reflection** – Your outer world mirrors your inner world. Shift within, and life shifts too.

We're manifesting every single day—whether we realize it or not. And as you can see, it takes more than just hoping and wishing. It's about clarity, alignment, gratitude, and inspired action. The inner creates the outer.

The Importance of Protecting Your Energy

One of the biggest lessons I've learned over the years is this: protecting your energy is not optional. It's *everything*.

Looking back, one of the things that never felt quite right in nearly all my relationships was that our energy just didn't match, especially on a soul level, we were not aligned.

My spiritual practice means the world to me. I've seen the ways I've co-created with the Universe—both intentionally and unintentionally—and it still blows me away. But here's the truth: It takes effort every single day. That's why it's called a *practice*.

If you're like most people, you probably have folks in your life who feel entitled to share their opinions about what you *should* or *shouldn't* be doing. I'd talk about manifesting in past relationships, only to hear dismissive comments like, *"Well if manifesting worked, I'd be a millionaire by now."*

That kind of energy? It drains you. It comes from people who don't get it—and worse, don't *want* to get it. And when you let that energy into your space too often, it starts to pull you off your path. I caught myself second-guessing what I *knew* in my gut to be true, simply because I was letting their energy override my own.

When someone isn't aligned with you energetically, you *feel* it. You shouldn't have to shrink, filter, or compromise the way you show up in order to be with someone. That's not your person. Period.

I stopped meditating. I stopped doing the things that kept me grounded and whole. I allowed months to pass without reconnecting to the very practices that have always brought me home to myself—again, that was on me. Just like skipping workouts because I was too focused on spending every moment with him.

Those days of letting it all slide to prove my worth? They're done. I've reclaimed my space, my practices, my energy. And I won't give them away again. That is self-sabotage.

Brianna Wiest wrote:

"Here's how you know someone will betray you. Those who cannot fix their own life will often end up breaking yours. This

law has shown up again and again in my life. And you'll see it too. It's always the ones stuck in the same place year after year who become the hardest to be around. They tend to expect the worst and turn small problems into big ones. But those who are moving forward, well, there's a different energy around them. They carry intention. Because someone who's stuck in a self-destructive life will eventually destroy the good around them too."

Let that sink in.

The Importance of Celebrating the Contrast

I'm truly grateful for everything that's happened in my relationships—especially the last one. That deep, aching need I had for validation and love from someone else became the very steppingstone to finding it within myself. I've moved through the hurt and anger, and now I'm able to stand in gratitude. Gratitude for the contrast. Because now, I know what I truly want. I know what I deserve. And bare minimum? It's no longer on the table.

Everything around us is always teaching us—but only if we're paying attention. The Universe will keep offering the same lesson in different packaging until we finally get it. Personally? I'd rather not keep learning through pain and suffering. I want to get the message the first time. But even when we don't, the beauty is this: with every single breath, we have the chance to pivot. The chance to choose again.

Now, moving forward, I carry this truth: I am worthy of a beautiful, nourishing love. And if you've seen pieces of yourself in my stories, in my journey—please know this: you are too. You don't have to settle. Not ever.

Never forget how magical you are. No one knows your full story. No one sees the weight you've carried, the darkness you've moved through, or the mountains you've climbed just to be here. Your only job is to keep rising. To keep choosing yourself. And to keep shining—because the magic inside of you is already enough.

You are only *one thought* away from the shift. One *pivot* from despair to hope. One moment of *faith* away from calling yourself back home—to the truest, most beautiful love of all: You.

Final Reflection:

If there's one thing I've learned—and it's etched into every story I've shared here—it's this: healing isn't about becoming someone new. It's about remembering who the fuck you are.

It's about unlearning the lies we've been fed about our worth, about what love is supposed to look like, and about how much we're allowed to take up space in this world. It's about coming back to your truest self—the version of you that existed before the world told you who to be.

You're not broken. You're becoming. And every version of you that's existed—even the messy, heartbroken, self-sabotaging one—was just doing her best to survive. Honor her. Forgive her. But don't stay there. Choose yourself now. Love yourself forward.

You don't need someone else to make you whole. You never did. You've always had the power to give yourself the love, the safety, the magic, and the freedom you were looking for in someone else.

So, here's your reminder: You are worthy. You are powerful. You are the love you've been searching for.

Now go live like it. Live hard. Love Harder.

Afterword

Thank you for taking the time to read *The Girl Who Cried Love: A Pivot to Self-Worth*. Writing this book has been an awakening. It was "supposed" to be my first book, but I wasn't ready then. I'm so grateful that *Unfuckwithable* came first—because I hadn't yet shed the weight of an airplane full of baggage. From old friends to old patterns, drugs, alcohol and long-standing beliefs I didn't even know I was carrying, I had to let it all go. I had to feel it, write it, release it.

This book? It became the biggest therapy session of my life. I've been spiritually growing since 2008. I've believed in the Law of Attraction. I've taught about it, practiced it, posted about it. But the truth is, I kept forgetting. It's easy to numb yourself—and I did. I was really good at putting the sparkle on, even when I was hurting.

And the feedback I've received while writing and sharing this journey has been overwhelming in the best way. I'm truly, deeply grateful. Still, there have been moments I've minimized my own pain, wondering, *who am I to write about hardship?* Other people have been through worse—physical abuse, relentless trauma, unimaginable loss. But that's just another way we silence ourselves. Pain doesn't need to be ranked to be valid. And I never showed it, not really. Only those closest to me knew what was going on behind the music and the lights.

The title of this book? It came from a somber, but kind of comical moment with my friend as we moved my stuff out of Columbus, Ohio. We joked that I was "the girl who cried love." But it stuck. I've been thinking about this book since 2006. It would take nearly twenty years, and one heartbreak after another, before I'd be ready to write it.

And of course, the timing of the Universe was hilariously divine. I didn't know how the M chapters would end. But the day before I was supposed to edit his chapters, we had *that* conversation. It was like the Universe whispered, *"It's time to let go, my love."* Only this time, I was ready to listen.

For the past year, I felt like that girl in the meme—kneeling beside her bed, praying for a sign, while the entire world exploded outside her window. I was *that* girl. And yeah, I even sent it to my friends, and we laughed because that shit was too real. Because that's how it goes sometimes. We don't leave until we're ready. Until we've gotten the lesson. Sometimes we get that lesson over and over again. And when it's time to go, it's terrifying, but necessary. But the reality is we can't welcome the new while still gripping the old.

I don't know how, or when, or who... but I *do* know what's meant for me won't pass me by. I have pure faith in that. I hope you do too. I hope you found pieces of yourself in this book—especially if you're in a hard season. Relationships are complex and layered and rarely black and white. Pick up any Esther Perel book, and you'll see what I mean.

I'm not a relationship expert. But I *am* pretty damn good at coming back to me. And I hope you get there too.

So, to the girl who cried love:

I see you now.
And I've got you.

To you, dear reader—wherever you are on your journey—here's what I want you to know:

You are worthy. You are lovable. You are powerful beyond measure. You've survived every heartbreak, every low, and you're still here. Keep going.

Music has saved me more times than I can count. The stage reminds me that I'm alive. That I'm home. And maybe your version of a stage looks different—maybe it's a journal, a canvas, a kitchen, or a quiet morning walk—but whatever it is, don't abandon the thing that brings you back to yourself.

And when you close this book, do one thing for me:

Go to a mirror.
Look yourself in the eyes.
And say, *"I love you."*
Out loud.
Let that be your next pivot.
Because you're only one thought away from a new beginning.
One breath away from reclaiming your magic.
One choice away from coming home to yourself.
You've got this.
And I'm cheering you on—every step of the way.

With all my love,

Lindsay

Acknowledgments

I'd like to thank my beautiful family for always being there for me. Chev, I love you bigger than the sky cuz the sky never ends. I am blessed to have such a huge support system in my life. Mom, I am so grateful for you. You've stood next to me through it all. Thank you for going through every word of this and helping me get it right.

Thank you to my best friends—Tricia, Brandy, Scooter and Angelic, Camo, Matt and Nicole, Sarada, both of my Jess's, Amanda, Elisabeth, Khris and May, Ryan, Kinsler, and Kristina—my Cold band family, Will and Celeste, and the entire Cold Army. Your love and support have gotten me through some of the hardest days, as well as the most beautiful ones.

To my amazing team at Best Selling Publishing: thank you for coaching me and guiding me through this process. To my publicist, Denise—thank you for your hustle, your vision, and your belief in this story.

A special thank you to all my favorite teachers and authors: Lewis Howes, Gabby Bernstein, Mel Robbins, Dr. Joe Dispenza, Matthew Hussey, Jillian Turecki, Esther Perel, Jay Shetty, Esther and Abraham Hicks, Eckhart Tolle, Michael Singer, and the late Dr. Wayne Dyer. Your work has given me inspiration and wisdom that can only come from Spirit. I'm so deeply grateful that you do what you do.

And thank you, Spirit—for co-creating with me, guiding me, and bringing all things into alignment at the perfect time.

To You, the Reader—

Thank you for being here. For holding this book in your hands, in your heart, and in your healing. Whether you saw yourself in these pages, cried through the memories, or found strength you didn't know you had, I want you to know: your journey matters.

You are not alone. You are not broken. You are becoming.

Keep rising. Keep pivoting. Keep choosing you.

About the Author

L indsay Manfredi is a musician, author, speaker, life coach, and truth-teller with a passion for helping others come home to themselves. Best known as the bassist for the platinum-selling rock band, Cold—with two gold albums under their belt—Lindsay has spent her life on stages and in the trenches—searching, stumbling, healing, and rising.

She is the author of *Unfuckwithable: A Guide to Inspired Badassery,* and her follow-up, *The Girl Who Cried Love: A Pivot to Self-Worth,* is a reclamation story—for anyone who has ever lost themselves in love, only to find something even greater on the other side.

A two-time TEDx speaker, Lindsay has spoken on the power of music and the transformative impact of organizations like Girls Rock Indianapolis. She is also a passionate voice for self-love, self-worth, empowerment, and radical healing. Lindsay is proudly endorsed by Ernie Ball, Jim Dunlop, Ashdown Engineering, Black Flys Eyewear, and Sullen Clothing Company, and has two signature series basses with Diamond Guitars.

When she's not writing, touring, and coaching, Lindsay can be found spending time with her friends, pouring candles, cooking, reading, seeing the bands she loves, traveling, lifting heavy things, and listening to all genres of music (except country) ;-). She's always practicing the art of becoming. She lives in Los Angeles, but her magic is universal. You can find her at www.lindsaymanfredi.com and on all the socials @lindsaymanfredi.